DAWN
∼ TO ∼
TWILIGHT

Also by Daniel Mark Epstein

DAWN TO TWILIGHT

NEW AND SELECTED POEMS

DANIEL MARK EPSTEIN

LOUISIANA STATE UNIVERSITY PRESS

BATON ROUGE

Published with the assistance of the Sea Cliff Fund

Published by Louisiana State University Press
Copyright © 2015 by Daniel Mark Epstein

Grateful acknowledgment is made to the editors of the following magazines in which these poems first appeared: *Agenda* (England), *America, The American Scholar, Atlanta Review, The Atlantic Monthly, Chelsea, Dalhousie Review* (Canada), *Georgia Review, The Hudson Review, The Kenyon Review, Little Review, The Michigan Quarterly, The Nation, The National Review, The New Criterion, The New Republic, The New York Sun, The New Yorker, The North American Review, OnEarth, Open City, The Paris Review, Per Contra, Poetry Magazine, Prairie Schooner, Raritan, Sewanee Review, Shenandoah, Southern Review, Southwest Review,* and *The Virginia Quarterly.*
"Miss Ellie's 78th Spring Party" and "The Sentry of Portoferraio" appeared in *The New Yorker;* "The Comb-Bearers" in *Poetry Magazine;* and "Climbing," "Cygnus Musicus," "The Follies," "The Inheritance," "Miami," "The Man Without Legs," and "Mannequins" in *The American Scholar.*
"Lady in Her Bath," "Madonna (with Child Missing)," "Miss Ellie's 78th Spring Party," "The Portrait," "Scorpio," "The Secret," "Song of the Beekeeper," "Song of the Hermit," "Song of the Sap Miller," and "Song of the Young Woman Gathering Ginseng" are from *No Vacancies in Hell* by Daniel Mark Epstein. Copyright © 1971, 1972, and 1973 by Daniel Mark Epstein. Used by permission of Liveright Publishing Corporation.

Designer: Laura Roubique Gleason
Typeface: Janson Text
Printer and binder: Lightening Source

LIBRARY OF CONGRESS CATALOGING-IN-PUBLICATION DATA
Epstein, Daniel Mark.
  [Poems. Selections]
  Dawn to twilight : new and selected poems / Daniel Mark Epstein.
    pages cm
  "LSU Press Paperback Original"
  Includes bibliographical references.
  ISBN 978-0-8071-6119-7 (pbk. : alk. paper) — ISBN 978-0-8071-6120-3 (pdf) — ISBN 978-0-8071-6121-0 (epub) — ISBN 978-0-8071-6122-7 (mobi)
  I. Title.
  PS3555.P65A6 2015
  811'.54—dc23

                                                                    2015006260

The paper in this book meets the guidelines for permanence and durability of the Committee on Production Guidelines for Book Longevity of the Council on Library Resources. ∞

For Sarah Longaker

Contents

Fin de Siècle, 1981–2000

New Poems, 2009–2014

Early Poems
and Vignettes
1967–1980

The Exile's Letter

I first left the cities behind, then
the crowded wheat fields, and last the women
because I couldn't bear their loneliness.
Far away they spin, behind me,
and the stuttering bells and hysterical sirens
speed out of earshot
wailing like deserted children.

Heaven still lies far beyond my means,
there are no vacancies in hell—
no goddamned place to go now,
not one blessed thing left to do.

And at this distance I'm no better
than a punch-drunk photographer, scrambling
in widening circles at a family reunion,
up and down on one knee,
telescoping the clustered generations
and defying their gravity.

Bodies crammed near static in the streets
await the plague winds of late spring:
cool air of death to stave off famine,

while I'm land-wrecked a few miles from water
feeling more happiness than they can know,
hoping that one straw of sunlight piercing a cloud
can prop the sky up for a few more hours.

Mountain and Tidewater Songs

I. SONG OF THE BEEKEEPER

My bees gather the last winter store
from smart-weed, Spanish needles, and goldenrod.
    I will have my cup right side up
        when the hives rain honey,
and men in town will pay for it.
        They are afraid of the sting.
When I'm wiring the brood-comb frames
        and folks ask my business, tell them
I'm stringing the harp for my bees.

2. SONG OF THE SAP MILLER

Give us a southwest wind after the frost
    to set my trees all tingling in the grain.
Sun draw the sap up
                frost keep it down:
    no sap before light hits the frost,
    no sap when the cold is gone.
Kettles hang in the granite arch,
       a blue stream of smoke twisting skyward.
Smooth-skinned young maples start with high spirit,
fair on a run and flooding the keelers,
but they won't hold out.
    Now my thick-barked scarlet ladies
        do not shy at my auger.
I'll sink the elder spiles no deeper
   than your sweet white wood
and tickle the juice from your limbs.

3. SONG OF THE YOUNG WOMAN GATHERING GINSENG

I've been hunting ginseng since dawn
    from Sang Run to Backbone Mountain
untangling brush under red oak trees.
This virgin bed blooms with the five-fingered leaves,
and the berries! A berry for every flower.
My skirt is full of the spiral trunks, some
heart-shaped roots for the heart, spindles
that grind well for herb tea. But you,
    little man, with your broad shoulders
and long tap-root legs, you will bring
a pretty penny in the Chinese market.
Some lord will bid high to feel you under his belt.

4. SONG OF THE HERMIT

Traveler beware, your cool grottos
hollowed in the world's side are my anterooms.

Sing clear of my range
or hear your song die fast on the air
like breath that clouds in the cold and vanishes.

There is no walking shadow in these hills
but mine. My dreams are singular.

Old Man by the River

Flood tide, boats glide high above the bank,
day lilies crane to look into the sun.
What kind of friends would leave me here alone,
an empty house behind me, a full graveyard
ranging from my door to the garrulous river?
Kind friends, and true, to leave me with my thoughts.
My teeth are gone, my hair's a white cyclone;
I have more secrets than heaven will ever know.
Take my daffodils, what a bargain of light
for the reckless April that discovers them!
Little girls with lightning-quick hands
arrest the leaping blossoms in mid-flight
and lay them on my doorstep in the night.
Today I scared the boy who brings the news.
I am a weathered man the adventure of whose
        conversation nature has immured.
Three walls are deadpan stone, the last is the river.
Who will I talk to when the river runs away?

Old Man at the Wood's Edge

Leaves, dry skirt of the wind, lie down by me
        and don't blow away.
Sky is low, the sun's in hiding;
        this masterless winter like a cataract
of broken days, has made
           a tombstone quarry of these hills.
The woods are full of skeletons and the closets
are full of orphaned saplings, birds
nursed in their chilled arms, perched
        on their white shoulders.

I made this cold in the raw image of my absence
so that I might know revenge for my own death.
It's a violent, senseless act, like most acts of love.
I hang the moon in my heart,
        sweep the sky of stars.
My children must learn to find their way in the dark.
I am a hard river, a misfortune
          without pity. When I go down
I'm taking the summer with me.

Lady in Her Bath

All day has been morning. Birds rattle,
        the trees stock still beneath them,
leaves blue in the white air. The girl bathes
        gracefully, her own epiphany,
all of cool circles in water.
Does a god move in her limbs or is there
a god in the air around her guiding them? Or
        is all light self-radiant?

She draws her body slowly through the pool
        bathing him from her, his flesh
and vision. It is this freedom
that is divine in her momentarily,
flash of her smooth limbs, white, whole.

The eyes are violet. Her eyes are blue,
        yet bathing, the bright sun
deepens them. The eyes are her own,
not violet for nothing. I will leave out the lips,
for these the light has forgotten.

The Portrait

Her face hung white and empty as a spoon.
    She had resisted every breeze and flutter
that shuffled dead air through the shutter,
    propped up all morning in a pose.
To flush the color from that stilted rose
    was more than he could do that afternoon.
Perhaps a slip of light would catch her breath.
She stared through every shade that touched her skin
    like a breathless doll or manikin.
So at noon when a bolt of live light struck
    her cheeks, he would rather stand and look,
The canvas stretched as blank and taut as death,
    for one so seldom pictures such a tint:
certainly nothing anyone could paint.

The Secret

She would not pick up stones
even the most beautiful ones
or keep them, let alone
keep them, they never look
the same on the windowsill, or in
a bowl as in the brook;
she would not
pick flowers either
and they grow
so much faster than stones.

Scorpio

I loved a girl who was in love with death
and made him a song she would not sing to me.
My child lay wound in a golden maze of bunting
in her arms, my gift to her, and a still-unopened rose.
These could not match death's promises.

"This year is as hard as life by our calendar,
with a black winter at either end of it.
Oh you that so flatter the mystery
but love your answers more,
if the earth should spin at random in the night
and this high room we lie in turn on its stem,
will you know dawn from evening when we rise?"

"It must be the strength of his arms,"
I said, "and eyes that never turn aside."

"No. It is his silent listening," she replied.

I loved a girl who was in love with death
and made him a song she would not sing to me
or speak, or hum, despite
the knot of promise in the boy child's limbs,
the spiral introversion of the rose.

The Follies

Blind Mr. Klugel loves the baritone of Mr. Cantini.

Mr. Klugel rocks on the back porch, listening
while his wife begins her nightly striptease
     in the bright showcase of her bedroom window:
a benefit for the ragged voyeurs of the South City
    who can look but cannot touch.

Time for all good children to be in bed.

From the tar roof of a row house over the wharves
    pours the wide baritone of the moderately drunk Mr. Cantini
singing the sun into a new country, singing
the boats to sleep in their slips, taming the oil rainbows
    to a flat shimmer in the harbor lights,
calling the stevedores to battle in dockside bars and blank alleys,
tuning up the full moon chorus of neighborhood dogs,
    summoning the sluggard moon,
waking up everybody's children.

Cash Only, No Refund, No Return

Earl stood on two legs when he had one to spare,
    then on one leg when the cancer got him,
a short leg and a wicked crutch.
By his own count Earl was accomplice to thirty-four
    murders, ninety-two muggings, and five suicides.
His finger followed the headlines in the paper
    spread out on a glass case that bristled with knives:
Florentine daggers, Arkansas toothpicks,
black bone and pearl-handled stilettos with blades
that kick loose and lock fast with a flick of the wrist,
Turkish daggers with serpentine blades
    to snake the guts from the meanest vendetta.

He stood there in the back end of the arcade
    and they came to him
from bars, the precinct lock-up, from flop houses,
whore houses, foreclosed houses, faithless wives,
good friends gone bad, betrayals, threats, divorces.
Earl had the voice and nose of Jimmie Durante
    and knew how to sell knives.
He just stood there behind the display case.

The Man Without Legs

The man without legs has huge arms.
He rolls himself along Park Avenue on a skateboard,
pawing the concrete with rubber knuckles.
Sparks fly from the steel wheels of his skates.
The man without legs is the quietest beggar in the city
and makes $225.00 a week after expenses.
He looks straight ahead.
He knows pity from the inside out.

Madonna (with Child Missing)

Shouts from the street, spotlights crossfire
at a third-story window. The woman
stares through smoked glass at a crowd
and firemen in glazed slickers—
flames climbing the stairs behind her two at a time.
She lifts up the window sash with one hand,
kisses the infant and rolls it out trusting the air,
the soft knock of skull on stone in her heart.

At the Millinery Shop

She wants what no clerk in the city can bring her,
    a hat that will make up her mind.
White satin speaks to the red in her cheeks,
    red satin to the white.
Blue crepe shades the clear well of her eye.

She wants a hat to fit her head like an idea
        so perfect only she could have dreamed it up,
a hat that draws attention to itself by disappearing
        and to the head by building on it
a profusion of silent worlds in incomparable colors.

She wants a hat that can think for itself,
        that will select the proper head for its household.
She turns her back on the round table-mirror
        and a garden of hats on spindles,
        admiring the beige lid with a feathery band.

Holding it at arm's length,
                her eyes half-closed,
she leans back
under a straw bonnet crowned with flowers
        that casually tries itself on her.

Miss Ellie's 78th Spring Party

Miss Ellie rattles the champagne glasses
like crystal ghosts that tinkle when they touch,
to hail the Main Line in for Spring
at the last minute. There isn't much
time to call the company to come;
this year she has forgotten everything.

Picasso's dancers shiver in a frame
next to the window. Spring as well
seems to have forgotten itself.
Several curios upon the shelf,
a lion and a girl in porcelain,
tumbled when an icy draft rained in.

She wondered for a moment who would come
this year; though she'd forgotten, who'd recalled?
She forgot again what day it had become.
All the tenses moved two ways at once,
past and present standing back to back
moved through each other with no deference
to Spring or Miss Ellie. She is young and old
alike and won't remember which is when.
The company will be arriving soon
                                    and then
everyone has gone off in the cold.

Fire froze in the chimney. The first cork
exploded from the bottles, aimed to blast
a marble frieze of Pan upon the stair
and everyone who ever was was there
to breathe the spirits moving from the glass.

Midtown Home

Snow falls so rarely nowadays and in the city
         you miss that sudden whiteness of things.
So when it started in the afternoon I was on the phone
         every half hour, arguing with the weather girl
and by dusk there was a good white layer on the streets
         and rooftops so that in the blue twilight
the city didn't look so much like the city.

And you need it that way sometimes, especially
         in January. I went out into it
         and down the corridor of alleys to the park
to watch the conservatory students
         slide down the walks and into the dry fountain.
The green bronze nymph was doing that backbend contortion
         in a coat of snow, the same way she does it

stark naked in springtime, and with leaves
on her breasts and forehead in autumn. The bronze
         war heroes were reserved. But I'm sure
they must love the weather as much as I do,
         and wonder why it snows so rarely these days.
I wasn't in such a hurry to get home, with night ahead,
         blue light turning to red and then yellow

city light made brighter by the snow,
and I was looking in one back window and then another
         all along the brick walls of the alley.
There was a square building with green shades in the windows
         making tall white frames of light.
And I saw through a crack the sheets and rails of beds,
but nothing in them, looked like maybe

a hospital supply house? I went closer and there
      on the nearest bed just under the window
was half a man's leg and a toothless mouth above it.
And his was only the beginning
      of a row of mouths in shrunken heads,
skins stretched thin and shining over sharp bones,
and limbs and the odds and ends of limbs, like

an ancient tribe disjointed in a higher world
      had spilled into the beds of this crowded home.
I stood trembling in pride and a deeper shame
that with all their futile suffering, borrowed breath,
I held more life in my body than they shared
      in that littered room.
They had no business being alive on a night like that.

In a Free Country

In a free country I would be shot for my thoughts of you.
Where thought was free as radio waves
        my mind would broadcast your outrageous beauty.
Naked phantoms of our wild nights
        would take every mind by storm.
In your name the slaves of industry and commerce
        would revolt, cops would strike,
truck drivers walk off whistling from their loads.
All creatures of the earth would drop their pants
        in tribute, they would fornicate pell-mell,
every man, queen, woman, dike, and child.
The old would have the young, every mother her son.
And I would be hunted down, my brain quarantined
        in a free country, thinking these last thoughts of you.

How to Survive Heaven

I was touching her where she'd never been touched.
The devil was in me. I said:
"If there is no more to heaven than this
    I am as good as a dead man."
And she said: "What did you have in mind?"

So I opened one door on a white blizzard of stars,
    and one to an avalanche of green that was our spring.
When I opened a third we lost our solitude
      to a grey parade of souls come down on a rainbow.
"You think big," she said, "beyond immortality and bliss."

Then this lady, with a wisdom beyond her years,
(I'm sure that she has been to heaven before
    and knows the ins and outs)
gave me fair warning:
"Lie to the angels about your dreams

      or they will confiscate them at the gates
and banish them to the bedrooms of the world.
If there are ghosts around us, love,
    they are dead men's dreams
no saint could smuggle into paradise."

The Late Visitor

A lady comes to me at an ungodly hour
and takes off her clothes,
she takes off my clothes. She sits
impossibly calm in the pouring light
of a lamp outside my window.

She reminds me we were immortal,
sloughing our worn skins
every spring, until
one beautiful woman kept her flesh
for fear a lover would not know her.

My lady casts no shadow.
She is clear glass
for inquisitive spirits.
The mirrors in my house
will have nothing to do with her.

Night Medallion

My woman is sharper than new truth,
        a clean bullet hole in thick glass.
Winter cuts its teeth on her, the sun
        cuts its hand on her,
she's too hot for the beach, the golden sand
    goes all to white crystal under her.

She's so proud, the full moon is her mirror.
When she turns from me I see her face
         in the rolling window of heaven
and when she comes barefoot to my bedside,
        holding a candle,
an elf skates on my heartstream.
Eager candle, milk my mind of treasons.
She's young and I want to fill her with the world.

Poverty

You call to me as if I were in some other bed
    or gone gold digging with the sun. In fact
I was dreaming I had ten minutes to haul a fortune
in jewels and coins from the cache of a secret mountain.
An underground river bolted under my boat,
    spilled the loot and rushed me back here penniless.
All I could bring home you're holding now
    in your hands, the rippling wings of my proud rising.

Tired of small secrets, little gifts,
    I conjure this secret mountain between us.
Behold the range of my discretion, even in dreams
    when you challenge me from every wind of the compass!
You call to me as from a tall house gratefully burning
    while fortunes panic around us, fall like stars.

On a Winter Morning

Running for the bus
I ripped my hand open
on a parking sign.
I was bringing you roses.
They were shivering
in green tissue
in my left hand
when my right caught
the blade of a misdemeanor.
My knucklebone smiled
like a beaten fighter,
then the blood came in bracelets.

I treasured them in the tissue,
swung aboard, paid my fare
and passed into the aisle
of faces shining
on my new hand.
Old men and young girls
stood up for me, offered
their old and new blood,
the family jewels
of America, priding themselves
on my deep color.

Their eyes said
*take what you need to see
from us,* their arms said
take what you need to walk,
their lips said *our bodies
are full of what you wear
on your white sleeve.*

After the Wedding Party

A white-faced mummer bride
      and bridegroom antic for the crowd.
They hope the mock veil and stovepipe hat
      will decoy what spirits plot
love's ruin: dead fathers, bygone lovers,
      imps of cross-purpose
that twist the sheets and spoil a mother's milk.

And so God speeds the newlyweds:
Hell's guard is down, they steal away, like
sly heroes at the crossroads in old westerns
      who get down and walk
while villains chase their riderless horses.

But the lovers have more than clowns and God
      to thank for their freedom.
The groom's mother
      has taken the devils on herself.
They flutter in her lace bodice
      like young crows.

The Dance

Fast clouds, in a big hurry to rain on somebody,
    but there's blue sky enough for us.
October trees, out of their minds with color,
and you and me like nothing else alive,
    cosmic accidents spawned between better judgments.
How can we bring a child into the world?
Everywhere people are starving, loveless, climbing walls,
and here we're hugging and kissing in front of God and everybody
in a park full of cheering trees
and our baby is doing a popular dance in your belly.
There isn't room in our bodies for all this joy!

The Catch

Under the dome of hemlocks
a green pool
where the creek breaks
its fall, a boy kneeled
fishing. You were afraid
our baby might spoil
his catch with her singing.
Then you were amazed
at his concentration
on the red bobber
and the sly shadows
that streak like trout,
the fast wishes
a boy mistakes
for the game of his mind.

I'm not superstitious
but I wondered if
the violet butterfly
haunting us in circles
was the soul
of that child's curiosity,
too polite and shy to make
eyes at you openly.
When you lifted your blouse
to feed our daughter
I know he saw that,
the round white gift
he is too old to cry,
too young to sing for.

He reeled his line,
took off for higher ground.
When I looked again
there was a man
his father's age
who smiled at us unabashed.

Summer House

1

Miles from town the long arm of the world
pursues me in the disguise of rivers and meadows—
a cheap trick she plays but I have to laugh
    and go along for the ride.
Same light and wind and wind and light,
      heroes who make the history of the day.
Clouds exiled from northern storms
      glide out from the nape of a mountain,
white targets on a shooting gallery range.
Ladders of getaway light drop from the clouds.

2

Old eagle mounts cross-drafts over the pines
      circling for slow rabbits;
young hawk scouts a ravine for challenges.
Sheep strum a field of waking daisies,
      pluck spikelets of couch grass;
day lilies chafe high collars of dagger fronds.
Mad architect pitched my roof at the world's end
and like Noah I want to bring everything into the house,
      at least a photo and a name for each,
light for my walls and a spell against silence.

3

But something resists, Great Nature or my little one
like a rich man's mistress embarrassed suddenly
by her position in the scheme of his affections.

When power drives the body to acts of love,
        love takes the first flight out.
And the best company, like the worst, arrives uninvited.
There is the heart's desire for a full house and then
there is the danger of friends as the leaves of the forest
        veiling the dance of naked trees,
the skeleton with whom you must at last lie down.

4

When mind is coterminal with nature's body
they hum like spent lovers in a bed of silence, rich
        as suspended applause, or counsel
so wise and potent we reserve it for ourselves.
Such full loneliness presages cordial death.
But this house reminds me I am far from home.
Men in strict training for a meaner death
        keep to themselves like this
in solemn imitation of their enemy, hoping
he'll think they're part of him and pass on.

5

I would be a better neighbor to the unknown
if I could round up the vagabonds of my world
and take them on the road with me when I go
to some ghost town that has forgotten
the jugglers of the wind, the high-handed clown
of sunshine, the stallion of love that leaps the hoop
flaming eternally between my life and death.
Surely we're allowed to take what we can carry

and maybe my show would bring children to the streets
and women to the windows of that sleeping town.

6

Night has slipped under the blanket of the lake.
Tideless waves throw wings of light on the sandy floor,
        nerve on nerve of gold underwater birds.
Earth's historians, wind and light, protect their sources.
But I'll bet wind comes from the spaces dead men leave
        and raw light rises from tombs.
Too gothic perhaps, but I swear
there is no greater truth in the storm and sun
whose riddles surround us like the horizon
no man can see without turning his back on it.

Fin de Siècle
1981–2000

The Date

Just as you were about to step out
in your sleek, black-sequined dress
fresh from the second-hand store, veteran chic
as only a fifty-year-old dress knows how to be—

just as you pulled the shades down by the ring
and shut the door, as you were walking
toward night and the rest of your life,
a lover, a quiet place where you might find one—

just as you stopped for the passing car
that braked so the boys could whistle as
you kicked back your leg, looked over your shoulder
to check if the stocking seam had run askew—

just as you passed outside the bar I saw you
as you saw yourself in the turtle-shell compact,
making sure it was the same you as left home—
just then you thought of my words, felt warm inside—

and now you must stay with me forever.

Lateness

Because the past cannot bear to part with her
the present suffers. So we wait
in a lobby under the eyes of chandeliers,
in train stations, on a street corner,
and at midnight in the graveyard with a spirit
who waited in this world and waits in the next,

for her October hair and bright May skin
have taken since the beginning of earthly time
and will take forever. Time goes with her;
wherever she stops the moments turn and spin.
Little minutes are doves eating out of her hand—
but when the hours call she does not answer.

Because her worth is beyond question or value,
kings have died for her and worlds collided,
skies caved in and hills leapt in the blue.
Her touch can melt the icecaps, make
buttercups flash in the desert, and wild daisies.
Poets have climbed to Heaven, singing her praises.

It isn't for spite she keeps you waiting there
at the small end of night's telescope. No,
it's not to belittle you with your bruised corsage
and trail of crushed cigarettes, left behind,
your shadow of beard, the useless theater tickets.
You are probably the farthest thing from her mind.

Maybe a street singer took her by surprise, or
the pattern of a scarf, scarlet and pearl-grey
made her pause and muse in the window, then
the moon would not let her go until it passed.

Maybe later in the street, admiring children
circled her on skates and led her away

laughing, into a wide park where it seems
her gentle protests failed as she tried on
their silver wheels and showed them whirling figures
they had seen before only in dreams.
Because of this, and the endless flattery of twilight,
the gay breeze beneath the sad story of each star,

she must honor the times that make her beautiful.
And the wonder is not that she is late tonight
but that anyone has ever seen her at all.

The Glass

Arc of flying horses, lily fan,
earth-rooted seeds that flower in the brain,
and now this woman
with all the tricks of nature to multiply
leaf upon leaf and heartbeat upon beat,
has come to live in my mind, as if
the world were not wide enough to hold her beauty.

I see her every hour of the day.
Nights are not long enough, nor the halls
of dreams where we pass on the way
to the radiant memory of passing.
Darkness is not enough, the single gift
the underworld provides us while we live,
to serve as a background for fantasy.

Restless with nights and dreams
she has to stand
up white as a diamond lightning struck
in broad daylight, between me and the world.
When she walks into the room something must break,
mind's image meets her coming with such force.
My glass is shattered and I cannot speak.

The Rivals

Happiness, in the fairy tale, comes hobbling
disguised as a hag. And the prince takes pity
on her, bringing her to bed, not knowing this

is happiness, thinking this is just a hag who
for some moral he values beyond comprehension,
has made this trial of his magnanimity,

and no sooner does he embrace her than she
becomes an exquisite maiden
with no past and no future apart from his.

So a man I thought my enemy came to haunt me,
featureless at first, in the dusk of dreams,
then turning slowly toward the daylight

until at last, in profile, I recognized
my old rival. He will have his revenge,
I thought, sending that face, more hideous

than anything of nature's cruel devising,
to flame up in a wall of sleepless rage
between me and all that I must see to do.

And my God, I thought, this is like love
who taught me her lesson years ago, though
she was beautiful and this is a death's head.

My enemy came to haunt me, tirelessly
until desperate, I kissed him, kissed him
dead. Then he slept, long and beautifully.

Homage To Mallarmé

I. THE BARREL ORGAN

Since my Vivian left me
to fly to another star—
Orion was it, Altair,
or the pale emerald, Venus?
—I have loved being alone.

All day I sit alone, but
for the cat, and one poet
of the Latin decadence.
Since my woman has gone
I love the legends of autumn:

slow days of September,
autumn's prologue, the hour
the sun rests before it goes,
when rays copper the walls
and redden the windowpanes;

the slowly fading echoes
of the last hours of Rome,
those languid poems that come
before Barbarian cries
and stammering Christian prose.

I was deep in one of those
I love, whose patches of rouge
thrill me more than the rose
flesh of a budding girl, and
plunging an idle finger

into the cat's black fur
I heard outside my window
the melancholy singing
of a barrel organ. Under
the tree whose leaves in spring

seem dreary since Vivian
passed by for the last time,
I heard the sorrowful engine
that turns dreams to despair.
Then I heard it murmuring

some cheerful, vulgar reprise
that once made the back streets gay.
Yet the tune reached into my soul
and called the tears to my eyes
as no ballad has ever done.

I sipped at that song like wine
and would not go to the window
to send down my coin ringing
for fear I might see the organ
was not alone in its singing.

2. THE WATER LILIES

That flaming July I had gone
searching for water lilies and the friend of a friend's
estate. Gliding along the reflection
of a double landscape, rowing through both I ran aground on
this clump of reeds in midstream, my dawn voyage ending
in mystery
where the stream swelled to a fluvial thicket, and a pond
wrinkled though unconcerned
by the indecisions of its spring.

Closer inspection revealed this
green barrier in the current concealed a low arch
of a bridge that flowed into shrubbery,
enclosing lawns. I understood. This was the park of Madame
X, the unknown chatelaine I had come to call upon.
The nature of
a lady who would seek out a retreat so damply im-
penetrable must be
to my liking. Surely she had made

an inner mirror of crystal
shielded from the glaring indiscretion of her days
and when she appeared the silver willows,
leaf by leaf, would shimmer in the limpidity of her gaze.
Bent as if under a vast weight before the stranger
would come to speak
I smiled at my easy enthrallment to the feminine
possibility, that
I might be enchanted by anyone.

Then a sound, scarce audible, made
me wonder if that lady would divide my leisure, or
hope against hope, was it the stirring pool?
The footfall ceased. O subtle secret of steps that begin and fade
leading the mind here and there as they wish, aswirl in
petticoat lace
flowing as if to surround the will in a watermark
by which she makes her way
heel and toe under sweeping brocade!

Does she know why she paused? Is it
to keep these reeds and my mind's drowsiness between us
veiling lucidity, holding above
my head the very mystery that confounds me? "O lady,
to whatever ideal your features conform, I fear
their precision
would ruin my deepest pleasure in the rustling of your
arrival, a certain
charm defenseless against invasion."

Separated, we are one. I
mingle with her in strange intimacy, in this sublime
suspense afloat where my dreaming delays
this hesitant lady more than any number of suitors
could do. How many idle speeches would it require
to discover
so intuitive an agreement as I contrived in
order not to be heard?
Now my will rests on the scales of time . . .

O my dream, tell me what to do,
render in a glance that virgin space in solitude
as in memory of this place I pluck

one of those magic water lilies that suddenly rise up
enclosing with hollow whiteness a perfect absence
made of new dreams,
of the joy that will never be and my breath held in fear
of an apparition.
I leave with one, rowing in silence

slowly, so not to break the spell
in my flight by casting a ripple toward the shore
where anyone coming might discover
in foam or bubble a clear simile for the abduction
of my ideal flower. Yet if the lady comes, drawn by
apprehension
something strange has occurred, if the lady, that wild, proud,
or thoughtful lady should come,
so much the worse for the ineffable

face I shall never know! I pushed
off and was skirting a bend in the stream homeward bound
bearing away my fictitious treasure
like some glorious swan's egg from which no flight will ever spring,
swollen with nothing more than that emptiness of pure
self, exquisite,
a lady pursues down paths of a tidal garden, pausing
now and then on the edge
of a spring to be crossed, or a sound.

3. OLD TIMES

Spiderwebs on the casement,
the wardrobe is ancient too,
fading curtains, peeling chairs,
nothing you own is new.

Didn't you wish, my sister,
with a glance at time vanishing,
my poems might set in meter
"the grace of some fading thing?"

New objects displease us
and scare us with their cries;
their need to be worn out
taxes our energies.

Come close that German almanac,
the days it proclaims are dead.
Lie down on the threadbare carpet,
calm child, pillow my head

on your knees in that faded gown
and I will talk on and on
of old clocks and cracked furniture
till the fields and streets are gone

under the cold of night.
Are your thoughts wandering?
On top of the casement
spiderwebs are shivering.

Champagne

All the angels that might fit
    on the head of a pin,
every spirit with its petty sin
    must pass through here
        on the way to bliss.

They appear out of nowhere
    in silver chains
rising through the clear crucible,
    and scatter in the gold
        to dance for us,

then at the crystal heights
    burst into chorus.

The American White Pelican

Calmly afloat some distance from the shore, the pelican
　　　　has been taken for a sail,
its moist feathers glistening in sunlight.
A large flock flying is a seraphic sight, wings beating
　　　　in unison, without
apparent effort. After a few strokes they coast
in faultless arcs, often at miraculous height.

Honeycombed with air cells, they cannot plunge from the wing.
　　　　But the orange skin hanging
from its bill may be stretched in the service
of gluttony, driving the small fry into shallows
　　　　as they arrive with the new tide
to prey upon flies and gnats caught in the rise
and lower life swirled in the drift washing seaward,

the great fish schooled to shadow the small, eagerly
　　　　heedful of taking life in
order to sustain it. All seabirds know this
and the time of its coming. Now the white pelicans
　　　　that have been patient in a line
along the beach, steal into the surf, then
so not to fright lugworm or gudgeon, smoothly glide out.

Some distance from land they scud into line in stern accordance
　　　　with the sinuosity
of the beach, facing shoreward awaiting
their leader's motive. Then all is commotion: the birds
　　　　flailing the water with white wings,
throwing it at the sun, plunging their heads
in and out, and stitching the blue to a lace of foam,

advance in a boisterous phalanx filling their pouches
                    as they go. When satisfied
with the catch, they wade and waddle into line
upon the shore again to rest, standing or sitting
                    as best suits them, leisurely
swallowing the fish in their cheeks. Then they rise
in a flock, circling high in the air, for a long time.

The white pelican builds upon the ground, a nest of sticks
                    and twigs upon sage or sedge,
a home with low walls of sand around to guard
the chalk-white eggs, whose surface is rough to the touch
                    due to the shell's irregular
thickness. The idea that the pelican feeds its young
from a wound the bird has gashed in its own breast

has no place among the facts, though it endures.

Cygnus Musicus

Note the scale of tones that flies from a brass bugle
        and, trusting that Nature creates nothing in vain,
compare the horn's shape to the windpipe of a swan,
        that snaky tube of bony rings. You see
the bird's instrument is altogether equal
        to playing the music praised in antiquity:
those plaintive strains, a cello-like requiem
        murmuring through the reeds its prophetic sigh
as death waves the swan toward asylum where
        no one may hear him sing, no other bird
break up the sacrament of his dying hymn.

Also in the windless glow of a sea-beach
        they sing before sunrise, says Oppian.
Pythagoras was so moved he began to teach
        that the poet's soul in death becomes a swan
so his divine harmony will not be lost.
        One night before Plato came to Socrates
the sage dreamed a swan hid in his breast;
        and hours from execution the swan sounded
to him like a joyous prophecy of the Good
        waiting for us there in the next kingdom,
and not some hyperbole of bestial dread.

Now it seems the swan's melodic gift is fading
        or one must be dead to hear it. I have stood
long hours by lakes and estuarine rivers
        and recall only a stridulous braying, though none
of my subjects was ever summoned by Death,
        the singing master. I will go on straining
my ears in the twilight between hope and dread

I shall catch that mythic descant of the swan,
out of my senses at last to hear the singing,
like a father who hears the voice of his lost son,
that supreme fantasia, the soul's returning.

Caesarean

for TJE, born on Memorial Day

Startled from ancient sleep in a dark house
    by crashing walls, harsh torches, strangers
dragging him naked through his mother's blood,
    what hero would stand up to the invaders
with such dignity as you showed
    this morning, the first day of your life?
At the shock of air you cried out loud
    in sight of the new world, and a world lost.
Then you were quiet, curious, engrossed,
    blue eyes half-open bearing a ripple of light
from that primordial ocean cast asunder.
    May your vision never weary of the sight
of this strange country and our stranger ways.
    May the days be worthy of your wonder.

The Code

I took my son from his weary mother.
I gathered him up and paced the living room
in a grey sunrise crossed by early lightning.
After a little while he stopped his crying,
lifting his head from my shoulder to look around,
widening and narrowing his eyes
as if the world were stranger than it is to us
who puzzle over a lifetime of strangenesses.
My face, to him, is a luminous mystery.
He's not old enough to know just what he's seeing
(I wonder if anyone ever is) but already
he seems to know the code of sound and rhyme.
I heard the faraway murmur of spring thunder,
and my son smiled at me for the first time.

For a Child Frightened by Lightning

First night in our summer house the sky is falling,
breaking away in wide panes that crash in the valley.
And I am watching from an upstairs window,
thinking that thought is next of kin to lightning

when it crosses my mind the boy in bed below
may wake in the arms of terror and a strange house
while I am spellbound by one pine stallion
rearing at a low cloud bridled by lightning.

Then a bedspring creaks and my son runs crying
through darkness streaked and stunned, where I catch him
at the stair in midflight, hold him still running
from the beast that fled the hills to rage inside him.

Now that my child's heart is a study in thunder,
how can I tell him it will not call his name?
Nothing will calm us now short of sunrise,
gathering flowers where the sky has fallen.

Miami

After years of stock-car racing, running
rifles to Cuba, money from Rio, high
diving from helicopters into the Gulf;
after a life at gunpoint, on a dare,
my father can't make the flight out of Miami.

Turbojets roar and sing, the ground crew
scatters out of the shadow of the plane.
My father undoes his seat belt, makes his way
up the aisle, dead-white and sweating,
ducks out the hatchway, mumbling
luggage was left at the dock, his watch
in the diner. Head down,
he lurches through the accordion boarding tube,
strides the shining wing of the airport, past
windows full of planes and sky, past bars,
candy machines, and posters for Broadway shows.
Gasping in the stratosphere of terror, he
bursts through the glass doors and runs
to a little garden near the rental cars.
He sits among the oleanders and palms.

It started with the Bay Bridge.
He couldn't take that steel vault into the blue
above the blue, so much horizon!
Then it was the road itself, the rise and fall,
the continual blind curve.
He hired a chauffeur, he took the train.
Then it was hotels, so many rooms
the same, he had to sleep with the light on.
His courage has shrunk to the size of a windowbox.

Father who scared the witches and vampires
from my childhood closets, father
who walked before me like a hero's shield
through neighborhoods where hoodlums honed their knives
on concrete, where nerve was law,
who will drive you home from Miami?
You're broke and I'm a thousand miles away
with frightened children of my own.
Who will rescue you from the garden
where jets flash like swords above your head?

The Sentry Of Portoferraio

Blame this island town for the broken boy
who keeps his watch high on the falcon fortress.
Blame this town of rose and sea-green stone
stairways, and the daredevil swallows.
Was it not enough that beneath a circus of birds
his eyes should blindly fix upon each other?
Born lame as an old joke
did he have to grow up in such a town
of pinnacles, one cocked leg
cursing the steps that lead him to his home?

Accuse the snake in the cactus, fig, and grape
gathering liquor from the rainless air;
scold fish heads in the monger's stall,
cats on the sill. Charge the parents
of sturdy children whose eyes renew the horizon,
whose legs conquer mountains and pines.
Did we not conspire in narrow prayers
to divide his share of health among us?
Did we not invest in our cross-eyed sentry
suffering enough to make a nation wise?

It is the fury of providence
to crowd a family of pain into one creature,
then crown him guardian angel of a town.
It is his lonely insistence on Heaven
that leads lovers to the sudden view
of their bodies broken beautifully against themselves,
that leads our village skyward to command
an ocean, rise and stand up to the sun!
But somebody has to pay for the hobbling climb,
somebody has to pay for his double vision.

Climbing

When he gave up mountains he became
a window-washer, hoisting himself on block and tackle
fifty stories above the street. For the love of heaven
    is an addiction like stealing
fast time from the round jail of the clock.

He loves high windows. Saves them for last,
looking down on the traffic, crawling workers
whose vision he rinses clean as fresh glass.
Pigeons swing like puppet birds under his hands.
    But does he think downward?

Does he love his fear of the lurking flaw
    in the scaffold, the crack in a faithless plank?
Does he think of the fatal journey
    between his living and his death? No.
He looks in on the nodding accountants, winks

at an astonished secretary who drops her file.
He looks out along miles of reflected rooftops,
    the sky mirrored in the invisible window.
It is like flying on the surface of our lust
    for a visible horizon.

By noon the top windows are clear as a sudden answer,
    at dusk pure gold,
by night they are pure moon blue.
Sadly he rides the elevator down
and starts again at the foot of the blind wall.

The Carpenter

Old enough to know her father's need
for sleep, she would not wake him with her cry.
Through quartered window glass the cold
rides on the moonlight flooding her room,
casting a shadow cross on the bare wall.
She would not cry although the light seems cruel

as winter, cutting through the quilts and sheet,
tightens its grip on her legs. The pain there
thrives on, though raised in the dull heat
of summer when fever with a brutal hand
yanked the legs from under her, folding them
back to kneel as if she must pray forever.

But something stirs her father. And he turns
in his own pain, wakeful, knowing her awake,
leaves his bed and climbs the narrow stair;
rising toward the moon in the window beside her,
he sees her speechless eyes and smooths her hair.
He pulls a chair up to the glass that shines

in its beveled skin of ice. A single fingernail
rough work has left intact, becomes his tool
scratching on one quarter of the pane: a flower.
His daughter smiles to see it bloom in silver
on the moonlit wall, the first of a full garden
where two lovers are walking hand in hand.

It has been years since he has known
this freedom of making, since necessity
bartered plane and chisel for his pen.
He moves on to the second pane, a woman rocking

a child, its curled hand reaching for her lips,
her hair bound in a low hive but for a strand.

His daughter's eyes are moonwide now, yet calm,
eager for the next image. His cold hand
etches on the third pane a fine rose window
and altar rail where a young woman is kneeling,
her dress and petticoats ruffled like a peony,
under the priest's blessing, her first communion.

Smiling, she nods. One pane is frosted blind.
He cannot think to move his hand; it moves
as her eyes close, rescued from this vision:
he draws a hill and road that winds behind
where men and women vanish two by two,
climbing in slow procession, following, what?

The sudden heat of breath and hands has made
a rainstorm on the landscape—his work is done.
He kisses her asleep. On the stray fringe
of frozen light from the golden mural he gropes
his way downstairs, thanking the full moon,
knowing the sun will never be so kind.

Schoolhouses

The staircases are always last to go,
winding into the sky like cries of defiance
against the wrecking ball and dynamite.
And the "up" staircase is still adamantly "up"
though bells are silenced and the rushing students
have all passed on, and "down" is "down"
although there are no more classes above or below.
No matter. Imagination, delighting in space
as does memory, climbs and runs downstairs
stopping to rest at a landing, take in the view
that finally escaped the narrow windows.
It whispers: In this room I learned
numbers refer not to things but to what we think
about things, and down that hall
I fell in love for the first and longest time.
Here I discovered uranium. There, an honest man.
Here I learned the shortest distance between two points
is sleep. There I learned I would die, but not when.

Before the school was leveled it was abandoned
and served as an altar
where the neighborhood children celebrated
their rage against learning. My daughter and I
used to go walking there
to check on the vandals' progress,
windows newly smashed, legends of graffiti,
chairs dismembered, the clock with twisted hands,
books read by rain and fire, their spines crushed.
There is no vandalism so inspired, none so pure
as children's rage against what has loved
and failed them. It is a bitterness of heart.

I want my daughter to see the school
as mortal, nothing like a church.
I came upon one chapel in the woods,
abandoned but intact, the steeple
piercing an overhanging bough,
wrens in the belfry, the rose window
casting its roulette of sunshine
over the scattered pews. And in cities
where the Church has long ceased to serve
the parish they will sometimes comfort the ruin,
board up windows where stained glass was stolen,
consecrate the door with a wreath on Christmas.
Teenagers sneak into the nave, to make love
or drink wine in the enduring sanctuary.
But the school is mortal. Vandals sentence it
and wreckers come to carry out their will.

Now the low cedars press against the wind
in a field that was once schoolyard
and my daughter clings to my hand.
She doesn't know where we are. She
is afraid I am telling the truth:
the school *was* here that now is gone,
and home, bed, mother, father,
are equally frail and liable to disappear.
We circle the site and I am pointing
and explaining—rubble, rubble—
wondering whose locker held the bomb.

How many teachers slept with Valery Strauss?
What are the prime numbers after ninety-seven?
Why is the school more eloquent in this state

than it was in its stern glory when we were young?
And why couldn't the vandals have been entrusted
with the wrecking of the schoolhouse? That
would have been more practical, more humane.
Are they too anarchic to do the job right?
Is it the nature of vandals that
they cannot deliver what they advertise?
The original Vandals were passionate and thorough.
I read about them in Ancient History.
They overran Gaul, Spain, and North Africa,
invaded Italy and sacked Rome, destroying
many monuments of art and literature.
The schoolhouse vandals are sneaky, picayune,
anonymous, unworthy of their name.

Why do I take such joy in leading my daughter
on the outskirts of this animated emptiness?
What have I learned in school but the savage joy
of asking questions that brought the building down?
Why have I had to grow old to ask such a question
as why do we have to grow old to become wise?
I suppose I would rather be young and foolish
and probably am, though you'd never know it
to see my grey hair. Joy made me grey.

Mannequins

This indecent procession of the undead
    invades the Avenue windows, dressed to kill,
sporting tomorrow's clothes and yesterday's faces.

One struts in a velvet shaft of midnight blue,
       slashed down the back in a diamond heat of lust,
gold crown at the wrist and throat, a garnet ring.
Here Lucie Anne side-slits a terry dress
      trimmed in Venetian lace
and petal edging on the camisole. There a lady
      most unladylike, lounges
in silk of liquidly drapable muscadine,
      grinning the wine-red of wickedness. Another
borrows the schoolgirl's kiss, the cupie bow,
eyes round and empty as pots, and the apple cheek.
For we also yearn to join the innocent in their clothes:
      Jill in her jumper, Johnnie in his jeans,
sheep in their fleece, the pig in his narrow poke.

But I prefer them naked, the posturing frauds,
free from any trace of shame, and without nipples
      or the fur that friction-proofs our parts for love.
I like them headless, oh Marie Antoinette,
      what beauty knocked in the executioner's bucket!
I like them wigless, as a rack of bullets.
I like when a leg is kicked out of its socket
or an arm flings back in some preposterous gesture
as if to say
"So happy to have missed the agony of meeting you,"
or
"We who are early salute you from the backs of our heads."
I love when the feet swivel for a fast retreat,
and the head jerks in wonder defying the neck.

65

But when they are assembled and decked out,
they turn vicious, whispering through the glass:
"How have you achieved your shabbiness?
Where is your glamour, the youth you were born with?
Where, if you have one eye, is the other,
and if you have three limbs, where is the fourth?
Where is your hair, marcelled or carefully windblown,
your eyebrows, the artfully painted lips?
Put your face to the glass, you wretched snail,
kiss me, you desecration of a man."

At Poe's Grave, Westminster Church

Lovers tread lightly the April grass,
Whisper among tombs, in honor and fear

Of the very souls that might bless
Their passage. This green island

Necropolis in the urban sea
Invites lovers to stroll,

Embrace out of sight of all
But the gentle dead who cannot

Hide their delight, but spin it out
In myrtle, sudden violets, wild thyme.

The stone lyre wound in laurel
On the cornice of the poet's tomb

Cannot keep still in this breeze
But hums an ethereal chord as

The young woman leans to touch
A stone carved with her initials.

Her lover picks a violet for her,
She raises her lips to his and as

They kiss the breathless landscape runs
Lengthwise through them, vanishing

Into a niche where there is no death,
Past or future graveyard, no dominion

But the bound and indivisible soul.
When at last they come to themselves

Years later—or maybe only a few seconds—
The world returns to April somewhat shaken.

Gifts

I gave her a golden locket
  To shut my portrait in.
She filled it with a butterfly
  Wing the blue of Heaven

And wore it until the day
  She turned to me from the mirror
To kiss, and the locket behind her
  Opened and flew away.

I gave her an antique ring
  Some lover had lost in pawn.
She gazed from the sea to her hand
  One night—the diamond was gone.

I gave her a chain of flowers
  That die before they are old.
She will outstay diamonds and gold.
  I will give her nothing but flowers.

Lost Owl

When the sky is right, the moon and stars
Shine through the window on my son's bed,
Lighting his way to sleep. But last night
He called to me: An owl, he said,
Was singing from the oak tree in our yard.

An owl, I wondered, in this city where
All species are more or less endangered?
"Go to sleep. You must have heard a cat."
"But look!" he cried. "There is the bird!"
So I got up to sit with him in the dark.

On a high branch backlit by the moon
The pointed ears, the round head of the owl
Cut from the sky a perfect silhouette
Which chilled me even though it thrilled my son.
I sat with him in the darkness a long time

Charmed by his pure joy in the owl's song,
Known for centuries as an omen of doom.
What was it doing outside my child's room?
Singing, clearly, for a captive audience,
I in my fear, my son in glad innocence.

I yawned. The boy nodded. I tucked him in
And went to my corner of darkness, comforted
The patient owl that sang my son to sleep
Was not mine—the owl I dread—but his,
The kind prophet of a strange new wilderness.

Silence

When at last you would not answer me
I listened like a spy at Heaven's door
And conjured up a dawning, soundless country
Where thought became its own best orator;

Where crickets sang no louder than the moon
And starlight made more music than light rain.
O echo of an echo, reverie,
Thunder tiptoed down from the soft mountain

Where I filled the air with love words once
And wrote in granite to outlive my age.
Now though I sweep the verses from this page,
The blank space cannot capture that silence.

The Book of Matches

Because I could not stay with her forever
The book of matches each red tip a year
Of marriage flared in the untidy cellar

Next to a bag of gift-wrapping ribbon
And paper which made a restless dragon
Breathing fire, licking the floor joists,

Burning craters, fountains of jagged fire
Up through the living room where the piano
Moaned in a crescendo of broken strings.

Flames climbed a ladder-backed chair, lit
Greedily on books, speed-reading the legend
Of our years together, disdaining the hearth,

Attacking the constancy of a staircase
We climbed one after the other hand in hand
Long after the children had gone to sleep.

Because I could not hold her long enough
The fire wrapped our bed in a cruel curtain
Where our bodies once shone making love

And at last it burst into the children's room
Furious to find them gone, no longer children
Any more than we are bride and groom.

Epiphany

Out in the cold, the contents of a house:
Carpets, lamps and bedsteads, kitchen range,
Holiday litter, bells and tinsel. Strange,
As if a huge hand lifting the residence

Shook it above the street while fingers probed
Corners and closets looking for evidence,
Clues among new clothes, toys, books unread
And games the children scarcely learned to play.

Who lived here last year, only yesterday?
Cardboard Santa and the Three Wise Men
Pause over the lintel to watch a star
Wink through a flawed cloud. Lost again.

Somewhere tonight a child is being told
There will be a better home for him
In the new year, a warm bed and fresh linen,
Constant love, and new toys for the old.

Helen

"Tell us a love story,"
Pleaded the class in chorus.
"Our lessons are all done,
Now don't lecture or bore us,"

They prattled, except for one,
Helen, whose gaze looked lost
In the maze of willow branches,
The girl the boys liked most

For the faraway blue of her eyes
And brown hair straight as rain.
"Tell us a love story, please,"
They begged the teacher again.

He frowned and longed for the bell,
Saying, "All the love stories I know
End in heartache, or death—"
Then Helen, from the back row

Called at last from her daydream
In the voice of an innocent lover,
"Tell us a love story anyway
And stop before it is over."

The Twins

The secret of twins is that they have no secrets
But a code like the jargon of bees
Or the rushing of a creek through grasses
So what is known to one is known to the other.
Falling into step along the beach or boulevard,
Surrounded by light or shadowing each other
The twins project a harmony so perfect
That, to all of us born lonely, destined to struggle
As lovers, parents, brothers, reluctant strangers,
They are a mystery and mild reproof.
We dress them alike, angry over our strangeness,
Envying those blessed to be born separate and one.
On the green seesaw of their delicate incarnation
The twins balance, a perfect closed parenthesis.

The Boy in the Well

How brightly the stars shine beyond the day,
Men at work in town, children at school.
Birds twitter in a feathery mimosa
And ghosts visiting the abandoned farmhouse
Far from town, slip through the fingers of light.

Ding dong dell, Johnnie's in the well,
Deep in the farmhouse well, out of sight
Of all but God's curious, unsleeping eye.
He's fallen far from the wafer of light
Which hovers above him at the mouth of day,

Fallen down, down the green stone cylinder
To a moist hole where there are no answers
To his cries but his own echo or
A cicada maybe, the prophecy of a crow.
A rope tied to the windlass slipped.

Who put him in? It was his own notion
After the blind beggar in town explained
How from a pit delved deep enough
You could see the stars shining at noon.
So many nights lying on his bed, gazing

At Orion swaggering across the heavens,
The boy would dream he was in a cave,
Warm and wise, watching stars dance
Above the literal day uncommonly bright,
Constellations acting out the old legends.

Down in the well the boy thinks he hears a cicada
Or maybe it's the strange echo of his voice.
How brightly the stars shine beyond the day

Which by now has journeyed far beyond morning.
He wishes on one star with all his might,

That Orion might reach down and save him
Or wake him from this nightmare in his own bed.
He doesn't know anymore if it's day or night.
By now the children have come home from school,
All but the bravest. His mother will miss him.

Beauty and the Beast

He was drunk and twice my age,
The greybeard at the party,
Old enough to declare failure
As husband, father, and teacher.
And as far as I could tell
He was a failed poet as well,
Though his poems were everywhere.
He thought I admired him so
I would be charmed to be taken
Into confidence as he extolled
A beauty smoothing her hair,
Much nearer my age than his:
"She's the one, the one I know
Will turn it around for me,
The woman to save my soul."
I nodded in sympathy knowing
The obvious rule—the man
Who thinks a strange woman can
Save him, is his own doom.
I watched him lurch through the hall,
Kiss her hand. A perfect fool.

Ten years later they're married
And he's given up whiskey for tenure
In the Midwest. His wife I hear
Is more beautiful than ever
And kind, clever, and strong. He
Has made peace with his children.
And now that I'm older I open
His book from time to time to see
If I may have been wrong
About some of his poetry.

Bobolink

You rise from dry meadow grass
    With a laborious flutter, more
Wing-action than the shortness of your flight
    Would seem to call for

And so it seems obvious
    Flying for you is a steep effort
Nature exacts, though not without amends,
    Bobolink, reedbird;

The wiry tones of your song
    Set forth a waltz in clear whistles
At first, so well-sustained! But then you break
    Down the bars, stampede

Your notes into a reckless
    Song fantasia piped at lightning speed
No one can follow—not the barn swallow
    Who soars with such grace,

Not the bird-watcher stalking
    The field, not blind Tom with all his skill
At sound-catching, his passion for filling
    Darkness with music.

Ricebird, reedbird, bobolink,
    Your song is the strained apology
For all of the weak-winged, condemned to sing
    Because we cannot fly.

Magic for Houdini

After the feast in his honor, the magician
Checked his watch, blinked, palmed a yawn,
As amateurs turned water into wine or wine
Into water, and beamed at his applause. Next?
One held a cigarette paper rolled betwixt
Thumb and forefinger, and beguiled
The crowd with faultless patter promising
To turn this sheer paper into a live moth.

Gracefully, he rolled the paper. Smiling,
He made a fist. But then the Truth
Upstaged the actor, as it sometimes does.
When he opened up his hand again,
The smile that had been poised above success,
Died on his lips. Where life should have been,
A flutter of fresh wings as the moth flew free,
Death left its ashes, the poor bug's remains.

Knowing the greatest illusion ends in folly
As even the best magicians fail sometimes
To make the incredible act a certainty,
Houdini raised his hands to start a round
Of clapping to mask the man's embarrassment,
A simple trick of professional courtesy
For the thing boldly attempted, bravely lost—
And maybe a little sympathy for the moth.

But then the audience drew in its breath.
A living moth came flying from nowhere
And circled the mortified magician's hair
Once, twice, three times. Crackling applause

That might have come from pity came from fear.
And no one's dread ran deeper than the master's
Who was all too familiar with these powers
Of darkness. He would be dead within a year.

The Genie Makes His Peace

I do not recall who trapped me in that darkness
The world knows as a vessel of light,
By what cruel trick or Asian sorcery
I was sucked out of this life like smoke
Into that bronze flume, then knocked about
To serve some adolescent fantasy,
Borne down and upstairs, up and down
In a poor boy's hand. Sightless, I was aware
Of jewels glowing on trees in a dim cavern,
His desire, the mansion, the King's daughter.
And my magic would fetch him all of this,
Though I must be the blind slave to his master,
Free only to serve, benighted otherwise.

I don't know what my lot was like before,
Though it must have been a life of service,
Good deeds and example after a youth well led.
It is far too long ago, a man's age or more.
For when the boy had gained all he wished for,
The vessel that was my crypt got lost at sea.
And the tides shouldered me along the littoral
Many summers and winters, by sun and starlight
In view of cottage, belvedere, and beacon,
As I drifted out of time yet ever mindful
Someone on the beach might spy the lamp
Gleaming in spindrift, tangled in sea wrack.
I weltered, mured in dreams, longing and spite,
Blind rage over the world that was denied me—
Houses, wives and children, books and fame—
Redoubling the diabolical vow
If ever I saw the light of day again
I'd use the power solitude had won me
For vengeance against the masters, all vain men,

Even the luckless wretch who set me free.
Curse him, and stop his heart at the next beat.

Plans drawn in darkness fade in the daylight.
As I might cup my own cheek with my palm
To prove if the dream be real, my liberator
Rubbed the carapace of my little prison,
That coffin, the ship that bore me from the past
Onto this dazzling, unfamiliar shore,
The white caress of waves on the sand's thigh
Under clouds like tattered sails of galleons.
In this light I met a man as old as I,
As sad and bitter, who wished only to set me free,
And nothing remains of my passion but the pity.

The Inheritance

The night his heart stopped, and my father
Drove the Cadillac haywire into a shadow,
Nobody knew where he'd been. A heap of money
Lay strewn across the front seat as if Death
Had thrown it back in his face;
In the ignition dangled his cryptic keys.

My job: to find the locks for those keys
And what they guarded, a puzzle my father
Left scattered in his wake for me to face.
I had to open the doors under his shadow
Though one might easily open upon my death,
A scene of vengeance, or a vault full of money.

All we ever argued about was money,
His love of it, my disdain. Now the keys
To his kingdom fell to me, as if Death
Had longed to cast me in a role my father
Created, while he watched from a shadow
As I fumbled at entrances he refused to face

At the end. Weary, confused, he would not face
Any problem he could not kill with money:
Adoring women, the law's relentless shadow
That trailed him rattling chains and prison keys,
His failing heart, his curious son. My father
Knew he was dying and tried to buy off Death

With coin of the wrong realm. When Death
Laughed and threw the cash back in his face
It must have been that moment my stunned father
Saw the border of the dominion of money—

And love beyond. Too late to explain the keys
To me as I cried angrily after his shadow,

Too late for me to hear him, once his shadow
Faded into that crowd in the halls of death.
Without a word of advice I got these keys
To a dangerous treasure. I see his lonely face
Smiling upon my grief that all the money
I find won't buy a farewell from my father.

Father, open the door behind the shadow
Money cast between us, and then Death;
Face me, bless the bearer of these keys.

Collection

I rode a hundred miles in a limousine,
Gun in my belt to capture what was mine.
He knew what was coming. Held the door for me,
Poured the drink I knocked back spitefully.

I told him if he did not pay
Me what he owed I would take away
His car, his house and furniture, his land,
The ring from his finger, finger from his hand.

I told him if he did not pay
Me X amount of cash by Saturday
There would be no Sunday. I would take
One by one the weeks of his month away,

The days of his year the years of his life;
I'd take away his children and his wife,
All he ever dreamed or had not dared
Yet dream, that too, nothing would be spared.

He nodded. When I had gone out the door,
Leaving it open for the night to enter,
I wept because I didn't know for sure
What the man owed me, what I had come for,

Or how I'd lived without it for so long.
My rage was old already, the night was young.
Under the cracked laughter of the moon,
I ordered my patient driver to move on.

Russian Village Suite

after Marc Chagall

I. LISTENING TO THE COCK

When the world was still
Upside down in slumber
And trees seemed to hang
From the night clouds,
And the claw of the moon
Scratched between silences,
I heard the crow of the cock.
I heard the cock sing
And it was not for day,
Or for night he was crowing—
It was for life.
I heard him cry for
Dear life which was coiled
Inside him like a hen
Full of eggs while
High above in the night
The barnyard animals
All dreamed of living
The lonely lives of men.

2. THE REVOLUTION

O Nikolay, what a show
You have made for the crowd!
You are a living flagpole
For the banner of Revolution!
All eyes are upon you
As you play the acrobat,
Standing on one hand
While the flag waves from your legs!
All the world is watching,
Armies, children, and lovers
As you stand on one hand
On the table where a rabbi
Sits holding the scroll of the Law.
All eyes are upon you, all
But the rabbi's weary eye.

3. THE THREE CANDLES

Harlequin tunes his flute
To play for the wedding
A song of blood and fire,
A song to make the dead
Happily dance with the living.
Angels with violins glide
Over the chapel dome
Serenading groom and bride
As they walk above the earth.
A shady angel unrolls
The red carpet for lovers,
The living and dead, to dance
As they pass from innocence
On this path of blood and fire.

4. WHITE CRUCIFIXION

Lions above the arc
Rise up roaring in pain
As a tongue of yellow flame
Blows from the temple door.
Why is the temple on fire?
Why are the books on fire?
Why must a bearded scholar
Shouldering the sack of Time
Warm his hands at this fire
Of the white scroll of the Law?
Why is our village burning?
In the stream of Heaven's light
The flying dead hide their eyes,
Whispering at the vision:
One of their own on the cross,
His lean and tormented loins
Wrapped in a ragged tallis.

5. THE FIDDLER

When in the night the fiddler
Flies over the town
Scattering notes like silver,
Tuning birds to a chorus;
When in the night the fiddler
Crosses the strings with his bow,
The church spires stand on tiptoe
To listen, the whistling trees
Shake off the dust of snow;
The stars rub their eyes,
And shake off the night clouds.
And I wish I had three heads,
Three sets of ears to hear
The golden and green melodies
Of the fiddler as he goes by
Leaving footprints on the sky.

6. IN THE NIGHT

If God ever speaks to me
It will be on a night like this,
A snowy night in January.
We will be embracing
In the middle of the street
So dearly in each other's arms
A lonely man in his doorway
May warm himself at our fire. Yes
It will be such a night as this
That I'll hear God's voice,
A night when there is such light
From the knife of the moon
The snowflakes all around us
Tremble: stars taken by surprise.

Memorial Day

for David Bergman

The library is closed—Memorial Day—
We honor men who died for our freedom
In wars that most of us cannot recall.
On the corner, men who should be schoolboys
Flag passing cars to deal cocaine.
The steel doors of the library are fit
For a vault. No windows figure in the wall
To let light shine on the books,
Just glass brick pocked by bullets
From drive-by shootings, thick glass
Cracked in spidery traceries
Like promises shattered.
                              Light
From a million books burned in Berlin
Casts no shadow on the grey fortress
That is all this neighborhood will ever know
Of a library. Here the books are safe
But the readers are burning.

Equinox at Newport Farms

Winter deceived us. Now the March wind
Heckles the weatherboarding of the barn,
Drives the weathercock out of his mind.
Poor counterfeit! He can't tell North from South
Or night from day now they are equal and
The lamb's head is in the lion's mouth.

A heron or a heron's ghost in the mist
Wades the marsh, hieratic, Egyptian,
An elegant, high-stepping egoist
With the rare balance to stand alone
In cross winds, still as a bird of iron:
An emblem of long life, so I've heard.

Yet, pinned to the cupola, that painted bird,
Wind-drunk, sun-blind, man-made,
Will outlast him—and me too, I'm afraid—
An emblem of human thought awhirl upon
Its axis, fanning the compass for direction
While the world ponders, turning in precession
Of the equinoxes, framing an axial space
Like the veering spindle of a spinning top.

Winter deceived us, making us embrace
The long darkness, the hopeless horoscope.
Now something about this vernal equinox
Piques my Libra nature, my need to balance
Future darkness against the daily light.

Neither old nor young at forty-six,
I study the hunting patience of the herons,
The mad persistence of the weathercocks . . .

What days will come to equal the coming night?

Dead Reckoning

for Monsignor Joaquin Bazan

Halfway between the familiar harbor
And our destination, soon it seemed
Partway between nowhere and nowhere,
The stars we counted on to plot our course
Fled before a mass of ghostly clouds.
And there was nothing more to guide us
But the ship's log and compass,
A scribbled record of our starting out
And the wobbling arrow of direction,
Vague tokens of the past and present,
And the sensation of speed and distance
In the puffed sail, the rope in our wake.
As for the future: the vision of a coast
Unknown and indescribable seemed
The more precious the longer we were lost.
Day dawned upon fog as dense as night.
And some, after many days like this
Turn upon each other in blind rage,
Dive headlong from the foretop,
Or drown in grog, forgetting
Why we ever left home, signed on
For such a voyage, to a land unknown
When nothing had been promised beyond hope.

The Traveler's Calendar

Dawn opens the accordion of facades,
Formstone and striped awnings of a street
Robber Barons paved to lure the drones
Hived in textile mills along the Falls
A hundred years ago.
                          In my corner room
With a view of row-house cornices and
The ruined forest on the hill beyond,
I keep no clock or mirror.
I want no ticking image to remind
My muse of Time's progress on this front,
The dial of minutes or my quotidian face.
Nothing temporal excites this place
But daylight, nightfall, and the creeping dust,
Metamorphic wind against the glass—
And this eternal Traveler's calendar,
Months adorned by Currier & Ives.

Faithful as Christmas, the agent of doom
Sends me this quaint scroll from Connecticut.
You know the type: a paper monument
To Mark Twain's America, the cake-tin
Rococo sweetness of the Gilded Age.
January snow, the horse-drawn sleigh
Leaving the fields trackless, immaculate;
Skaters testing ice on the mill pond;
Children chasing butterflies in May.
If there is a naval battle in July,
You may be sure it happened long ago
When patriots died gladly for their land.
And heavenly smoke-billows from the cannons
Mingle with clouds to hide the fire and gore.
Always a merry steeplechase in spring,

Always the summer sailing on the Bay,
Cloudless, stormless, happy mirror of blue!
Farmhouses in the lusty light of morning,
Twilight stealing the green hills away;
The October perfection of still life—
Grapes and apples light cannot resist
Touching with silver fingers. Always
The glorious landscape larger than the man,
The boy forever fishing the mountain stream,
Innocent, proud, beloved.
                                        America!
Who could forgive or forget your promises,
America as it only could exist
In dreams of men who toiled to barter dreams
For a row-house mortgage, insurance premiums?
Humanity was lost in your vast mood—
A mood-mountain, longed-for, uncertain—
A troubled child that could not come to good,
His passions buried deep under the mountain.
America, who can forgive or forget you?
I revisit the past, I can and I cannot.
Our landscape is stricken, the waterways
Poisoned with chemicals I cannot name,
Our sunsets freaked and stained with iodine.
Nothing looks the same but the pure flame
Of sun at noon. I mourn what was never mine.

The Hartford agent wants to sell me "Life"
For what it's worth to him and my family.
His calendar's a subtle tug at my sleeve,
Or not so subtle, now that I study it.
As if the color plates were not enough
To signify the imminence of Heaven,

Here come the phases of the moon:
    January frames the infant's face,
The crescent moon of March a boy of ten
Who, in flowering June, is a young man,
Grey in August, white-haired in November,
Dimples worn to trenches in his cheeks.
Death has made my calendar a mirror,
Flashing the twelve disciples of long life!
Then to remind me of the odds against it,
Death, the engraver, shows me the full moon
Like life in its luminous moment of glory,
Star-crowned, or cloud-adorned, while nearby
Lurks the black mouth of the new moon, saying:

"Oh live for the glory of the round of light
Crowned by the stars in July, or cloud-haunted
In April; but bear in mind the black circle
Of the new moon sailing stealthily among
Your gaudy planets and constellations.
I am the dark round period that waits
Each day for the end of your sentence."

The Lion Tamer at 2:00 A.M.

The crowd is always on the lion's side
  Against the man with the whip.
They wish the spangled girl would slip
  From her spotlight on the trapeze
And fall like a meteor on the ringmaster.
  The inner eye turns glory to disaster.
Hard to survive this art, harder to please.

Always the danger there is not danger enough
  To kill, the spice the crowd prefers to love.
But do not call that preference cruelty
  Which is just human nature.
Great success leads all too soon to failure
  As men make nature bow unnaturally.
While I put old lions through their paces,

Fathers get bored, the children become restless,
  Hoping against hope I will be mauled,
For they have paid to see the risk, and want blood.
  The art they applaud side-steps violence,
And this is why they go home from the circus sad.
  How can I make a show with ten tame lions?
I'll need five rude savages to save the act.

The Third
Millennium
2000–2008

Vision at Dawn

for Robert Beaser

I

I was wide awake before the wind.
Bands of coral clouds upon the azure
Horizon, bright above the lagging sun,
Closed like a louvered blind
Before I found words for the color.
Was there no painter at the easel?
Was I the only one at his window,
On a sleepy street or field of frost,
Who glimpsed the passing miracle?
A lonely thought—chilling as a ghost.
I wrapped a blanket around my shoulders.

Maybe one of my children, or neighbors
Would telephone to tell me they had seen
What I remember now uncertainly:
The sky was layered gold, then it was grey
(Or sliced with coral-red, incarnadine?)
Before the sun came crashing into day
To waken the world to its common vision.

2

What Death reveals to you He keeps from me;
This is not cruelty but natural law.
The thought that no one else saw what I saw
Is brother to the darker notion
That what everyone sees I could not see,
And this is a heartache as one grows old.

There is the wide sky, the hill, the ocean,
The maple tree once draped in shingled gold
That now bares its skeleton
To host the crow when the songbird is gone.

The Pure Gift

in memoriam LME

On the hottest day that summer, a rainbow
Arced over the clock-tower of the brick pile
We call The Rotunda, a dying shopping mall
With a wilting grocery, a druggist, a flower stall,
A dozen half-lit vacant retail stores
And a crafts gallery. I had just bought
A jewel box, the lid a parquet braid
Of spruce and rosewood artfully inlaid,
With a comb of music teeth to play a tune
For one who might never open it to listen.

There is a clear-cut purity in the gift
Purchased with love that may not be returned.
I walked out holding the treasure
The clerk had gift-wrapped in white paper
And bound with ribbons, silver and turquoise
All cunningly curled. Then I looked up
And saw the rainbow vaulting the violet sky
Late in the rainless day, bold and unbidden.
No gold anchors the generous bridge of heaven.

The Final Exam

They had turned in their bluebooks and gone,
All but one, whose eyes welled with tears.
The teacher would not rush her. He was kind.
It was the end of the term, the end of autumn;
Yellow leaves tumbled, spun across the lawn.
Time to go home and leave the books behind,
The mysteries of life and human frailty,
Free will and determinism; "Buridan's ass,"
Which posed the essay question that came last.
The hungry beast was led between haystacks
Identically delectable, each a perfect feast.
But then a cruel fabulist had trapped
Him midway between temptations, so that
While he drooled he could not budge
Moment to moment, for he could not choose.
The sun had risen and set upon the wretch,
His wasted flanks and then a pile of bones,
Since the Middle Ages. Maybe the bright girl
Was grieving over this. *It is not a fair match:
Pitting freedom and fate against each other.*
And let none of us presume to fathom
What made the pupil and her young teacher
(Who wanted years enough to make him wise)
Forget the pen, the beast, the philosophy class.
At last he drew near and touched her shoulder,
And they led each other gently into the world.

Fleur-de-Lys

When sepals and petals look the same,
As in the tiger lily, we call them
Tepals, these bright blades of perianth,
Sheathing the tulip and hyacinth,
The blossoms that do not bother to put on
Green calyx beneath the corolla gown.

If all this is Greek to us, then
So it is. Most of the savory words
That make a flower: anther, stamen,
(Not pistil, which some Roman
Named because its style reminded him
Of his pestle, and his swords),

Were spoken by Aristotle and Phidias,
Long ago, by hero, virgin, and wench.
Much later came the tepal, coined in Paris.
Once the ancient gardeners were done
Spinning flowers from words, no one
Dabbled in such magic but the French.

Hope

In winter the crescent moon vanishes
So quickly in the blue, down the horizon,
Between the starry darkness and morning,

Like the hull of a ship without rigging
That I was meaning to load with wishes,
O not for me, my dear, wishes for you,

And you and you, my friends, all of us,
Such cargo as could only ride upon
The silver shell of that hallowed galleon.

I daydreamed, got bewildered by my muse,
Sun on the lace of frost, and fading Venus.
I looked up, and the reckless moon had gone.

Cataract: 9/11

Lately the world seems darker,
Especially in the evenings,
And I light more lamps
To see no better than ever
Familiar faces and things:

Wayworn works of Art,
Books known almost by heart.
Is this the cataract, what
The Romans used to call
A portcullis or waterfall

Descending to subtract
From the sum of my seeing?
A fine word for a hateful thing,
Though now the doctors say
They can lift the veil in a day.

Who takes joy in the word
For a blur that steals his light?
The power is its own reward
And a gift of second sight,
This joy to build a tower,

Without fear or self-pity,
Of words for the horror
That attends the end of light,
A castle to stand bright
In the ruins of a city.

The Comb-Bearers

Some windless nights on Narragansett Bay,
The inlet looks like a field of green fireflies
As multitudes of the luminous jellyfish
Called "comb-bearers" float to the surface
For no evident purpose
But to amaze the fishermen and scientists

Who know them only slightly, each one no more
Than a pear-shaped living sack of liquid
With skin thinner than tissue paper, a sheer piece
Of moonlight on the sea, so fragile
The least ripple may tear it
To bits. Calm evenings, the amber-green species

May spread out over a thousand yards square,
An island made of bright individuals
Who usually live in the depths, a zone where
Wave movement ceases. Only on nights
Like these do the comb-bearers
Rise, when the bay lies still as a sheet of slate.

Loveliest of sea beings, the color
Of spring arbutus or pink anemone,
As some pass beneath the surface of the water
The effect is of rainbow glory
More seductive than moonlight
To the naturalist who might try to scoop one up

Ever-so-gently in his fine net and
Hold it awhile in a clear beaker of brine—
Perhaps the giant of the race, "Venus's girdle,"
Come from the Mediterranean—

An iridescent ribbon
Which vanishes en route to the laboratory.

The advantage of their luminescence
Is unknown, being of doubtful value in
Luring prey. As for mating: it is difficult
To imagine that these delicate,
Melting creatures could sustain
The violence of lovemaking. Yet they make light.

The Frame

In the heat of writing about you
In a blank book, my special one,
I skipped a page, wastefully.
When I thought I was through,
Turning back to where I'd begun,

I noticed this white space,
Speechless, peaceful, pure as only
Silence ever could be
Or will be, ever again;
The hush after hard rain,

Of a rosebud blowing open;
The lull that comes darkly
After someone has misspoken
And nobody knows what to say,
The quiet that fills a room

When death visits the house,
As the spirit hovers in place
And grievers have not yet
Seen it rise above the bed
And turn the color of air.

In the rush to finish my verse
About you, I left a space—
An empty foursquare frame.
And there I saw your face,
More haunting than any poem.

Ronsard's Dream

O wouldn't I love to be the golden rain
Drenching the bare thighs of Madeleine
As she sleeps, or tries to, in the downpour;

Wouldn't I love to be the great white bull
Who takes her as she goes over the hill
In April, a flower amazing the other flowers;

Wouldn't I love to slake the thirst of lovers,
Play Narcissus, making the nymph my pool,
And plunge into her all night long;

If only then that night could be eternal,
And dawn kindly refuse to rekindle
A new day—and mine be the last song.

Alice

She had come to the place
Just shy of womanhood,
Seeing and being seen
Lovely of form and face,
That cannot come to good
Without some sheltering grace.

Men would stop and stare,
Then turn away, ashamed
Of what they dare not do
And where they might not go,
If madness could be blamed.
Free of pride and vanity

As if she'd been born blind
Or never held a mirror,
She passed in her summer dress,
So oblivious of her beauty
She might search for its likeness
Behind the looking glass and not before.

Obsession

I study the hours on an heirloom watch,
Precious hours marked with diamonds
That scatter the sunlight over the room.
Since you left, I am obsessed with time,
Unsure if it is my enemy or my friend,
Knowing that all suffering ends in time.
I wonder if minutes might be redeemed
To some purpose, palliative and kind,
By watching them pass under the second hand,
Or spill in a silver stream through the hourglass,
The wavering thread of sand creating
A pyramid of minutes from its domed tower,
Where a phantom finger gently pushes down
On the white drift until the hour is over.

The hands of the pendulum clock atone
At noon, point to the zenith where the sun
Looks down upon our garden. Alone here
I ransom an hour of daylight,
Hovering over the gnomon of the sundial.
I'm furious at time, which has no end
And no beginning, no heart or balm to heal,
Blind with grief, sun-stricken and unable
To tell by sight an enemy from a friend.

In Late November

Of the butterfly bush, whose purple flowers
The monarch and the swallowtail
Sipped in August, near my windowpane
(Such a wealth of wings and flower clusters
I could hardly see the grass, the trees)
Only stalks and branches remain,
And panicles tipped with russet berries.

Now I see everything so vividly:
The young woman on her hands and knees,
Planting the meek shrubs three years ago—
Three short years and thirteen feet below—
Told me the light was perfect here and so
The plants would thrive, just wait and see
How gracefully the flowers would bear wings.

I would see her when she was not there,
Then go blind, standing right beside her.
How could I begin to explain such things?
Soon enough the blossoms reached my sill,
A floor above her terrace flat. Too late
For her to see the wonder she had wrought
Or for me to tell her. She'd moved out.

I never dreamed these branches in full bloom
Would all but block the summer view below:
Garden, gardener and terrace door,
Casting a dappled shadow across my room.
I never knew that when November came
I would miss the butterflies so much
And see the world more clearly than before.

The Everlastings

In a stream of mid-morning winter light
The lavender spray your silver ribbon bound
Hangs upside down from a pin, as bright
As any blue we ever saw in the garden.
With such great gifts, I suppose you might
Have done the same with your strawflower,
Or "cupid's dart," any everlasting,
The fire amaranth with its scarlet leaves,
The globe amaranth, or "love-lies-bleeding,"
With its drooping tassels of red flower spikes
That feel like chenille to the touch.
Such names! Who but a heartbroken
Gardener would make up such a name?

Some ancient Greek named a pure fiction
"Amaranth," the myth of an unfading flower,
Never supposing you might make it real
By picking these blooms just as they open
From the bud, before light can turn them brown,
Stripping the leaves, hanging them upside down
In bundles like this one hugged by a band
Until the heat of hearth and home has drawn
The last pearl of moisture from the stems.
For love you left me the lavender, fragrant,
And kept for your own the crown of amaranth
By which, in keeping with an ancient spell,
You've turned immortal and invisible.

The Widower's Journey

In and out of the mountain,
I ride on the railroad car.
As the coach lights go down,
My inward eye recovers.
Day funnels into darkness,
Then tunnels to light again.
Across from me two lovers
Are using the gloom to kiss.

I am untroubled by this.
But something is troubling her,
I think. He is uncertain.
The future is dark to us . . .
A mercy! I long to say
(Too shy for the intrusion)
We see sorrows one by one.
But this is not my play.

He answers whatever she asks,
His smile overturns her frown.
Tragic and comic masks
Overlook the stage curtain:
One fears it will come down,
One laughs that it must open.
The train rolls under the mountain
Where all of us travel alone.

The Glass House

Where should I cast my sorrow
If not here beneath these maple trees
At the lake's edge, with a wishing stone
The cold weight of my heart,
Wishing what has come might be undone?
In the glass house of dawn

Where shall I cast my cracked pebble:
At my own image rising from dry grass,
Purple loosestrife, asters and goldenrod,
Or beyond, where black water limns a cloud
Rainbow-winged, like a truant angel,
Or drowns the sparrow on the bough?

His song goes rippling on in trills
No lake can trace or echo.
Like the morning mirrored in the gloom,
The fallen world defies the world of grace.
Where shall I cast my stone
If not at the dark portrait of my face?

Psalm of Pernette du Guillet

The night was so dark it had hidden heaven
And earth from me. To my despair,
At noon I could not see a human face,
Though I heard voices. So when dawn
Came rushing in, as if from nowhere,
With its thousand colors, and suddenly
I was surrounded by light, better late
Than never, I joined in praising the glory
That led a new day through the broken gate.

The Clockmaker

Time should be heard as well as seen,
Says the clockmaker, carving a cuckoo bird.
My wife gives the sick child his medicine.
Who said children should be seen, not heard?

I work all night until my sight is blurred,
At this abandoned craft that now is mine
For all the comfort folly can afford.
Time should be heard as well as seen.

I can't imagine what life might have been
Without the babies crying, had I preferred
The cloister or the study at nineteen,
Thinks the clockmaker carving a cuckoo bird

In hours stolen from sleep, pleasure deferred
For the sake of this obsession, a daft machine
That never can refund the cost incurred.
My wife gives the sick child his medicine

Praying he'll sleep soundly and be fine
Tonight or tomorrow night, someday. The third
Time he cried out wrecked my whole design.
Who said children should be seen, not heard?

I dreamed he lay so peaceful that the Lord
Himself believed the stillness was divine
And would not wake him, although my absurd
Clocks froze and went silent for a sign:
    Time should be heard.

The Good Doctors

July. Sage and lavender heal the earth.
And I haven't written a rag of verse
Since April Fool's Day, when the doctors
Told us an accident of birth, a stray gene,
Some rare glitch in the brain, ordained
My son would never reason like a man.
For me it was as if he had died,
Someone I had loved but never known.

Under those harsh lights, no one could hide.
Because he could not talk or ring a bell
Like other toddlers, put the peg in a hole,
They had divided body and soul,
Searching for the mind that binds us all.
And it seemed to me so cruel
This child, with a good heart and a smile
Everyone who sees must repay in kind,
Should lack sufficient wit to tell—
In this world of falsehood and delusion—
Good from evil, wise from senseless men.
It seemed dumbfoundingly cruel,
And I lost the cadence of a season
That April day in my grief, a broken fool.

Lullaby

I sang to each of my children
When sleep came too slowly,
The words of a mystery
In a haunting minor tune:
Open the door softly,
I've something to tell you, dear.
Open it up no wider
Than the crack upon the floor.
Open the door softly,
I've something to tell you, dear.
I learned it from a street singer
Who promised me the rest
As soon as he could remember.
Now I hear he has died.
So I may never hear
Who knocked, who was inside,
What one had to say and why
The other would not open.
And not one of my children
Entranced by the lullaby
Ever turned in my arms
To ask what was unspoken
On the edge of oblivion.

The Suit

My grandfather, nineteen years of age,
Falls from the pages of the unabridged
Dictionary where I keep him pressed,
A sepia print of him in his second suit,
A double-breasted serge. The satin tie
Flows from a knot held by a silver pin.
His second suit. The first, he bought
With six years of savings, pennies earned
As cabin boy, deckhand, and seaman.
The night he put it on and went ashore
Some shipmate cracked wise about the cut
Of the cloth or the man who wore it, that
Somehow one was unsuited to the other,
The one being too fine, the other crude.
Whereupon my grandfather swung at him,
And one blow led to another until the men
Whirled into a blur of fisticuffs and blood,
Fought until their clothing was in tatters.

So now he appears in his second suit,
Bought off the rack in Hong Kong or London
Just after the Great War. He's tough
And handsome, bright-eyed, proud,
Daring the whole world to call his bluff,
Cocksure the clothes don't make the man.

Grandfather's Spectacles

He was not a brawler, or vain,
But came up in a time and class
Where a youth of exceptional beauty
Had to prove himself—man to man—
Time and again. Nearsightedness
Made him half-blind; so at fourteen
He went stumbling to the optician
Who ground him his first pair of spectacles.
Amazed by the view, he walked the streets
'Til dark, taken by leaves, pebbles, and stars,
Then the grin of a bully who demanded:
Drop the "frog-eyes" or he'd die laughing!
And in that fight, the first thing broken
Was the miraculous invention
Of wire and glass that let him see
The world and the cost of clear vision—
Ground to dust in the streets of the old city.

A Sense of Style

And in this frame great-grandmother looks lovely
    In her high-collared satin dress,
So many buttons! A button for every sin, as
    They used to say, and the stone
Cameo brooch that has come down to you, my dear.
    Long past her prime she maintained
A sense of style though somehow free of vanity,
    Unlike the pastor, her husband,
Who perhaps from too much Ecclesiastes,
    The *vanitas vanitatum*,
Was so obsessed with this he would not face a mirror
    Or the dark art of photography,
Said he would die first, which his wife took with a grain
    Of salt, or maybe not—we still
Wonder. But at last she hired Brady and assistant
    To come to the rectory on
Such and such a date when man and wife were to be
    At home, to take their portrait,
For there must be one for posterity, for all
    To read their lineaments.

And as it happened this was the very day my great-
    Grandfather chose to breathe his last,
A sad day for his widow certainly, and one
    Of confusion, not least because
The photographer arrived with his glass slides and
    Black box before the mortician,
Whereupon she sat the beloved in his chair, propped so,
    And stood beside him holding his hand,
(See, he looks a little drowsy and ill at ease),
But she is smiling in that way they do
    In the old photographs, having to hold the pose
For what must have seemed an eternity.

Tornado, 1911

from a diary

The inquest was reported in the press,
Words of experts and eyewitnesses
Like me, one may read when I am dead.
She entered the schoolyard before class,
A frail blond girl, no better or worse

Than the rest of us, my mother said.
Kate shut the gate, put down her books,
Seemed about to join us on the swings,
Although she usually played alone.
Next thing we knew a gust of wind

That spun our hair and made a moan,
Lifted Kate Sullivan into the air—
Her arms extended as if to measure
An adventure of impossible breadth,
Her skirt blown out like a balloon.

The wind carried her higher and higher
As one who had been called to Heaven.
Surely the angel that drew her skyward
Would be kind enough to set her down
In this hard world or another, gently?

But it was just a funnel of wind alas
That turned her loose as quick and carelessly
As it had selected her from among us,
Dropped her from a height of thirty feet,
And the earth struck her without mercy.

After Whitman's "Lincoln Speech"

The cannons are all silent as the dead
Of that distant war, buried
Long ago, and their widows and children
Also entombed, burned, or lost at sea.
Now it all comes to this hazy distance,
Earth, fire, and water distilled
In autumn air, the gold of chrysanthemums.

In the jewelbox theater where I toiled
Two years or more in wonder and terror,
As soldier and wound-dresser, prisoner of war,
The footlights have gone out
With the damp-eyed ladies in velvet
And men in waistcoats looped with golden chains,
Vowing to reduce war to pure science,
Gone into Manhattan's twilight and endless sleep.

The stage where the poet mourned his president
Is bare. Where shall we meet such heroes,
So justly grieved by grief so eloquent,
Or strong-limbed courage in a digital age?

The Vanishing Oriole

Orioles, common as robins when I was young,
Are going the way of the passenger pigeon
Whose mile-wide flocks two counties long
(According to John James Audubon)
Wheeled and coiled like serpents in the sky,
Shutting out the light of the noon sun.
Now nobody alive has ever seen one.

No hue in nature matches the oriole's breast,
That bright cadmium orange, except maybe
Marigolds when the sun is low. And I miss
The bird's staccato mezzo-soprano,
His pitch, so round and rich, his syncopation.
If he has a fault, it lies in the desultory
Treatment of his theme, a predilection

For chattering preludes and fiddlery before
The main melody—a fine construction.
Half-done, he'll take wing, leaving us to wonder
Who will sing the last notes, and when
And where, and who on earth will listen,
As if there were no end to the generations
Of passenger pigeons, orioles, songs and men.

Photographer Unknown, Neuvilly 1918

The light survives, exploding the north wall,
Splintering the vault above the side aisle,
Beaming upon the immobile white columns.
The church, surprised by so much radiance
Shelters the wounded soldiers, dark as pews,
Swaddled in army blankets, all equal now
In their suffering—blind, lame, or whole.
Who can tell the living from the dead,
Who suffered in brave silence or cried out
For medicine or mother? Not the doctors
Bending over the bodies, or armed captains
Judging who was ready to march once more
Into the treacherous forest of Argonne.
Here the light has outlived the last man.

And what it saves is arbitrary, odd:
A spotted dog limping through rubble,
Some silver wickets of the altar rail,
A ladder angling from a chancel window,
So angels might visit if they pleased.
The altar is piled with guns and medicine,
And above it—as though art must have its say
Even now, in the ruins of a French town—
Hangs a life-sized canvas, a baroque scene
Of the Ascension. Christ hovers in the air
Above the stunned apostles, and His mother
In wide-eyed terror, calls to Him, "My son,
Remember me when Thy kingdom comes,
Leave me not long after Thee, my Son!"
For this was the seventh and final sorrow
Of the Virgin on earth, who then was left alone.

Iraq

I thought the war was wrong,
But stammered, tongue-tied
Between a howl and a song.
Not that the war was right
Or the men who made it just;
But to fight the good fight
Each one in his way must
Guard what he knows best.

I know the human voice,
Gruff on the battleground,
Viaticum, the widow's cry.
Among these is no place
For political poetry,
Which being both is neither.
Too exacting of humankind
To forgive the lawmaker
Or soldier his assigned
Fault in the disaster;
Too pure and tenderhearted
To bear the weapons of peace
After the nightmare has started,
A poet is unfit for this,
Being more and less than human.
I shall try again and again
To countervail chaos,
Not as a poet, but as a man.

The White Quill

I sit on a rude bench under the maple tree
Watching sunrise open up the garden,
Dry the dew from the lawn, then turn
My dark windows above to glaring gold.
High overhead a squirrel is scurrying
Back and forth on a limb, with twigs
And leaves in his mouth, just frantic
To finish making his nest in the tree fork.
A few lyrate leaves rain down on me,
Stems corymbed with winged samara seeds.
My mind is on the character and fate
Of the man who toils behind one window,
Cloaked in darkness, then by dazzling light,
His crimes, lies and folly, work half done.

Here I am and there I am at once,
Spectacle and spectator, audience
And actor in a play without denouement,
Although I know how every knot was tied.
He sat under this tree before he died,
A squirrel above him scolding:
Get to work, you fool, winter is near.
Listen, man, there's no one behind the gold
Windowpane. That room is now for rent.
Look up and see what's drifting down to you,
Gliding and twirling on the autumn air:
A pale feather, longer than your hand,
White from pointed shaft to silken vane.
What kind of bird would drop from heaven
Such a pure quill, too large to be a dove's,
Too small and late for your great apology?

Old Man in Sun and Shadow

Of all my worldly goods and society,
Nothing is left but a table and chair,
A lamp casting dim light on a dark book,
And a grinning skull that will outstare
My blinking gaze unto eternity.

I gave my house to the homeless,
My money and shoes to the poor.
If that brings them no balm or gladness,
They are no worse off than before.
I gave my friends to each other,
My enemies to themselves. I pray
No favor of God or man except
Sunlight and silence where I might find
Some way to slow the minutes of a day,
Save motes of hours from Time's wind.

What have I given that I should have kept?
What have I kept I should have given away?

On a Theme of Ronsard

We die, then the rolling tide of years
Sweeps our works away all in due time.
God alone lasts. Of the human loom
Not a vein or sinew survives death,
Not a thought or feeling. The remnants
Are loose bones quartered in a lonely tomb.

Soul's joy is to behold God's radiance
And study its source; soul has no essence
But in this restless contemplation.
Happiness has little to do with this;
It comes from making family and verses,
A home, a garden, decent government,
None of which can gain a line or limb
From dust of those whom death has sent
Below. Therefore the bodiless realm
Of the hereafter has no cops or laws,
No cities, jails, or theaters—no applause.

As for me: give me thirty years of fame
To revel in the light of the sun,
Good red wine and a woman for loving;
Let the Devil take the century of renown
After the sunken grave swallows my name.
Once a man has passed beyond the days
When he can be moved and not just moving,
What is left has no more need of praise.

Heading Home

I watched the miles, I saw my life go by,
A drumbeat of bare trees and frozen ponds,
Forlorn stations, ruined factories.
I must have dozed, my head against the glass.
Women I dreamed I would have died for once
Mourned me in a dream. South by southwest
Our train cleaved the horizon, pushed the sun
Toward somebody else's daybreak, while
Heaven and earth denied my day was done,
Painting a fantastic continent
Of cumulus and ether, air, and mist,
Real as any land to a waking man.
A wall of purple hills sloped to the shore
In fluted cliffs; cloud archipelagos
Edged with golden beaches jeweled a sea
Bluer than our sky. Had I missed my stop?
Now was I on my way out of this world,
Alone on the express to Elysium,
Lotus trees, the lost woman of my dreams?

Shadows deepened and the speeding train
Rolled on into twilight. Slowly then
I came to myself, cold, woke to the thought:
This is how it must be at the end of the line.
You cannot tell the water from the sky,
Mourners from the dead, or clouds from land.
The fire of the sun has tricked you blind,
And earth, air, and water join in one.

Codicil

Vain men postpone their wills
Despite all rhyme and reason
In the toll of the church bells,
Thinking to outwit fate—
Because no sensible person
Would trust his gifts to the state.

But this happens every day
As the superstitious scheme
To hold Death at bay
Delays the signature
Meant to rescue and redeem
Control over the future.

My children, I write to you,
Being of sound mind,
As far as a man can know.
I am not rich or poor;
I am neither cruel nor kind
But your thinking makes it so.

I gave you life and give it again
Each dawn, the earth and stars,
The wind, the sun, and rain,
The choice between good and evil.
I gave you sisters and brothers
To love. Think of me as you will.

New Poems

2009–2014

Autumn Song

Little flower, you live in constant danger:
Likely to be crushed under foot or torn by wind,
Sun-scorched or gobbled by a goat.

These October days streaked with regrets and tears
Are like you, brindled flower, as they bloom
And fade, harried by heat as much as by the cold.

Our ship sets out to sea, not with ivory or gold
In the hold, but with fragrant apples for cargo. Just so
My days are not heavy but delicate, fleeting and vain,

Leaving behind the sweet, faint scent of renown
That quickly will vanish like the taste of fruit
Passing from the tongues and hearts of everyone.

Apologies

I'm sorry. I thought you were someone I knew
Long ago—and yet you look the same—
A woman who believed she knew me too

In another life. Was it Rome or Timbuktu,
New York or Paris I first heard your name?
I'm sorry. I thought you were someone I knew,

Just now as I passed you on the Avenue.
And if you were first to speak, I would not blame
A woman who believed she knew me too,

For time plays tricks on all of us. What seemed true
Forever, stutters, fades, a guttering flame.
I'm sorry. I thought you were someone I knew.

Yet after so many years the ingénue
Who blossomed in my sight and then became
The woman who believed she knew me too

Would be old by now and wizened, not like you—
A beauty bound for love, acclaim, and fame.
I'm sorry. I thought you were someone I knew,
A woman who believed she knew me too.

My Desk

The blue-green shade of an Emeralite
Glows on its pedestal of tapered brass;
The tiny bell-flower of bronzed tin,
Dangling from the beaded chain,
Is the first thing I reach for in the dawn.
Voila! The silent and familiar field:
A pink conch shell in which the spider weaves
His web reminds me, listen to the sea
If you wish your small voice to be heard.
On the windowsill: photos of Graham and Poe—
The dancer cartwheels her chambered nautilus,
The poet holds his Napoleonic pose.
A weary God from the façade at Chartres
Nods, his heavy head propped on his hand,
Like a man after a week's work almost done.
The plane of the desk itself: a hieroglyph
Of scratches, gouges, burns in rude oak,
Forty years of scars. You would think this ground
Had served brave armies that shed real blood,
And not pale men of paper, pen, and ink.

My mother bought it at a rummage sale,
When she was forty, twice my age, and poor.
"I want a desk so strong it will outlive us,"
I said, a week or two before Christmas,
"Broad as the span of my arms and long enough
So I cannot reach the far edge of it,
A form that will bear the weight of love and grief,
One that will see me through the darkest poem,
Strong enough for me to dance on, when I'm done."

Orphan

What was I looking for in that room
Crowded with old books, shelves so full,
It seemed they could not hold another title,
Except where in places a weary volume
Leaned upon its neighbor's crooked spine?
Some dimly remembered novel or poem
I once read and loved, or dreamed of?
Either a real book or the book of dreams
A friend once advised me to record:
Write upon waking, the dreams will come
If you wait and listen, word for word.
And night and day must be reconciled
Like mother and father, parent and child,
Brother and sister, lovers who have quarreled.

Although I never did as I was told,
I have met the morning every day I could,
Shaken the darkness, come to the table,
Truly grateful for what fare was offered,
Bran or manna, ambrosia or bread,
A sentence, a tragedy, or a kind word.
And now, almost sixty and an orphan—
As nature would have it—I am the age
My father was when he died. Every day
Seems to me it might be the final one.
Pressed for time to make peace with the past,
I look for a book so broad-backed and strong
That it will stand up on the shelf alone.

Dawn to Twilight

Tomorrow morning while the dew is fresh,
Brightening the green fields,
I will set out in my car for the Eastern Shore,
Where I know you are waiting for me.

I will leave Baltimore, and cross the Severn,
The blue tidewater cut with white sails.
I will drive over the Bay Bridge as mist
Unveils the ships and barges far below,
In no hurry. I know you will be waiting,
Though I do not want to be away from you
A minute longer.
                         When I get to the village
I will take the left fork that goes north
Along the lane of red cedar trees, then
Park the car and walk—
Hearing nothing, seeing nothing, my hands
Clasped behind me, holding each other.

I will not notice the first stars of twilight,
Or hear the last songbirds of the day.
Night and day will seem all the same to me.
When at last I reach my destination,
I shall place upon your grave one sunflower
From the field across the way.

Sundown, Newport Creek

1

In the salt marsh near my ancestral home,
I know the constant transience of things.
The disc of sun nods at the close of day,
Blood-red, more blood than light. The hum
Of wind is not wind but the beating wings
Of silver birds frightened into flight
By the sight of an eagle. Nothing is quite
What it seems. The elements mingle so
In this place where wetland meets the sea,
I know all blood is my blood, the wind my breath.
And if I have no heart to hunt today,
My friend, it's not to slight good company
But because, in my mood, predator and prey
Have become partners in the dance of death.

2

Under the sway of a full moon
The creek tide flows high before twilight,
Lapping the mud flats and the shallow sedge.
The white egrets that stood or stalked
All day in the salt-meadow cordgrass
Or roosted, snow-capping the red oak trees
Of the far island, now have flown away.
The barn swallows will come swooping,
Skimming and grazing the black stream
To feed on the same gnats and flies
That make the fish take to the air
Twist and splash down, leaving targets,
Concentric circles visible from above.

How else can the hovering terns pick out
The shape or shadow of their prey
From the great height they must attain
In order to dive and plunge to the degree
Where the fish idles, oblivious to the eye?

Meditation beside the Nanticoke

As I lay down beside the Nanticoke
Watching that tidal river flow and wind,
Wave and ripple parting the marsh grasses,
Rolling on forever, making innumerable turns
As it runs through the countryside to the horizon
Pouring its watery soul into the meadows,

I shut my eyes and tried to envision the first wave,
The nascent pulse that came at the dawn of time
Out of the dark, flooding the earth. Every day
The river changes, as seasons, stars, and clouds
Pass over, and men ponder, and yet we call it
By the same name, the river, the Nanticoke,

After a tribe of Indians who once lived here
And fished and hunted by these banks, the rushing water,
The very same sound. Likewise, a man changes
In body and mind: I sleep and wake and will not be
The same tomorrow, my body's strength and health,
This body which time shortens and consumes,

As winter gnaws the days, will not be as it is.
And yet my name will follow me to my grave,
The echo of an echo my mother first uttered
Will hover in stone above my ashes never changing
Although I am no longer the man who lived here
And passed through these bright stanzas singing.

Fireflies

After sundown you see the first
Out of the corner of your eye, then another

In the middle distance, the gloaming,
Where a grove of maples conspires,

Darkly thinking night-thoughts
While these inklings of light multiply

Glowing only as they ascend,
As if the effort to rise and shine dulled them

At a preordained height
No higher than a child's head, or

So it seems, while there is daylight enough
Bending along the broad curve of the sky

For us to glimpse the fading world they ornament.
Within the hour we can see a hundred

Bearing messages to the departing day.
They are supposed to be mating, soundlessly.

And if they were a chorus they would crescendo
At the climax or quintessence of twilight,

The instant that is neither day nor night.
After that the fireflies make themselves scarce,

Having no love for the deeper shades of evening,
Except for the brave few who astonish us

By rising above the treetops in darkness
Where one might be mistaken for a star.

The Music Lesson

My sixteen-year-old son at the piano
Is teaching me how to tell the tones
And intervals between the white notes,
Playing the keys ascending and descending:
The unison, the harsh second and sweet third,
Then the perfect fourth, more difficult, so
He sings a mnemonic: "Here comes the bride,"
Then for the fifth he sings the same words over,
Here comes the bride again, a tone higher.
And I wonder if I'll see him at the altar
Ten years from now, or twenty? I strain to hear
And get the interval right. He has the eyes of his mother,
My former bride and wife, brown eyes,
Patient and mild. The boy is a natural teacher,
Knowing the key to knowledge is to share it.
When he turns to face me I see in the dark center
Of his eye the image of his aging pupil.

Some Angels

Lying on their backs, looking up at the sky,
The boys have made angels in the snow.
Eyes to heaven, with heaven looking down,
They wave their arms like wings, while seraphs
In the clouds bless them with their winged arms.
The shapes they leave behind are lovely.
But more wonderful still are the footprints
I saw on the blue hill an hour ago.
A brief trail of delicate fairy shoes
Started out of nowhere in the field
And ended a stone's-throw distant, maybe
Left by one who longed to feel the earth
Once more beneath his feet and touched down
Briefly before starlight called him home.

He Wanted to Travel

He wanted to travel, but at journey's end
Found he was bored and out of sorts at home.
Alone in his study, walled in by his words,
Solitude weighed upon him like the tomb.

He wanted to go to sea, but the seafaring
Between life and death was scary, and so
He preferred the pleasure of tilling the soil,
But soon was scornful of the ploughman's toil.

What madness overwhelms the restless mind
That wanting all is satisfied with nothing
And doubting all, is foolish, hungry, blind.

He worked to master the arts and sciences,
Fiddle and paintbrush, math and chemistry,
And learned nothing, really. He wanted money,
And dug a mine but found the gold too heavy.

What madness overwhelms the restless mind
That wanting all is satisfied with nothing
And doubting all, is foolish, hungry, blind?

He longed for God and haunted church and temple
Like the lost ghost of a priest or a rabbi;
He wanted a soul and looked into the sky
Until it cracked with lightning and night fell.

Who Is the Stranger Who Overtakes Me

Who is the stranger who overtakes me
On a dark street and taps me on the shoulder?
I turn and there is nobody there but me,
And lights go on in the house on the corner.

I am familiar with the moment of waking,
Sometimes from a dream, mostly from pure silence
And darkness. But I have never been able to discern
The moment when sleep descends

And takes the book from my hands, the light
From my bedside table, my lover's hand
From mine. It is a mystery as unfathomable
As Death, which I suppose will be as gentle

And fleeting, an angel-guide for the lost ghost.
I shall wonder about these things forever
Like a child winking at the mirror, trying
To catch a glimpse of myself with my eyes closed.

The Late Sleeper

Under a blanket the color of blood
His dreams are gathering, unread. In a room
Vaulted like a gatehouse, the narrow bed
Launches the late sleeper to his doom
At the speed of light, through star meadows,
Like a glorious comet the restless children
Watch wide-eyed from the dormer windows.

Notes

Readers of my individual books since 1973 will notice the absence of the longer narrative and dramatic poems that contribute to each volume's composition and color. I thought that it might be an intriguing exercise to choose lyric poems from those books, in roughly chronological order, and see if those poems would tell a story of their own. Once I began going through the books and arranging the pieces, about a hundred, I was surprised by the extent to which these shorter poems, irregularly autobiographical, now emerge as a unified autobiography.

In this edition of my poems I have preserved the orthography of the original publications. From 1967 until 1987 I capitalized only proper nouns and the first letters of sentences, as one does in writing prose. From 1988 to the present I have used the older poetic convention of capitalizing the first letter of each line. This practice has little to do with the content of the poems, as the reader will see, but a lot to do with the construction and integrity of the individual verses.

Early Poems and Vignettes, 1967–1980

"Madonna (with Child Missing)" (p. 17)
The title comes from a broken medieval sculpture in the Walters Museum of Art. I read about the tragedy in a Baltimore newspaper in the early 1970s.

"At the Millinery Shop" (p. 18)
A friend suggested that I omit poems with extreme anachronisms; since the poems are rooted in time and place, it would seem unfair to history to subject this book to such a criterion. The title of this poem and its subject comes from a painting by Edgar Degas in the Chicago Institute of Art. A milliner is a hat-maker, and a millinery shop a store where one purchases hats.

"Miss Ellie's 78th Spring Party" (p. 19)
The Main Line is the western suburbs of Philadelphia, comprised of towns such as Merion, Ardmore, Haverford, Bryn Mawr, and Paoli, all of which are located along the Main Line of the old Pennsylvania Railroad. The train runs northwest from central Philadelphia parallel to Lancaster Avenue. The area includes some of the wealthiest neighborhoods in America.

"Midtown Home" (p. 20)
Until the twenty-first century one could telephone a weather line twenty-four hours a day to hear the weather forecast, which was updated hourly.

Fin de Siècle, 1981–2000

"Homage to Mallarmé" (p. 42)
These poems were inspired by the prose poems "Plainte d'automne," "Frisson d'hiver," and "Le nénuphar blanc."

"Cygnus Musicus" (p. 51)
The swan here is no relation to the real bird, Cygnus Musicus, the Whooper Swan of Europe and Canada. The myth of the Cygnus Musicus in antiquity was based upon the notion that a creature so beautiful ought to make beautiful music.

Third Millennium, 2000–2008

"Ronsard's Dream" (p. 113)
My verses are roughly based upon the erotic quatrains of Pierre de Ronsard's "Le Premier Livre des Amours," 2 (XX), "Je voudroy bien richement jaunissant."

"Psalm of Pernette du Guillet" (p. 120)
The poem is a close translation of the untitled "La nuit était pour moi si très-obscure . . . ," written by the poet Pernette du Guillet (c. 1520–1545). She is said to have been the real-life inspiration for Maurice Sceve's sequence of love poems "Delia: The Paragon of Virtue." She died in her twenties, her work unpublished. The "broken gate" is my embellishment.

"A Sense of Style" (p. 126)
It was not uncommon during the early days of photography to photograph the deceased as if they were alive, sometimes in the company of family members. Posing for pictures required the subjects to sit still for minutes while the exposure was completed. A man who was ill, or simply uncooperative, might have the decision to be photographed taken out of his hands.

"Tornado, 1911" (p. 127)
A similar incident was reported in the *Yorkshire Observer* of February 25, 1911. The report was subsequently redacted by William Godden in *Symons Meteorological Magazine*, 46:54, 1911.

"On a Theme of Ronsard" (p. 134)
The theme appears throughout Pierre de Ronsard's works—which are among the greatest treasures of the High Renaissance—but is especially focused in his poem "À Philippes Des-Portes, Chartrain. Elegie," published in 1587.

New Poems, 2009–2014

The title poem, "Dawn to Twilight," is inspired by Victor Hugo's famous "Demain, dès l'aube" ("Tomorrow at Dawn") and is dedicated to my mother. My companion during the writing of several other poems, including "Autumn Song" and "Meditation Beside the Nanticoke," was the unjustly neglected contemporary of Pierre de Ronsard, Jean-Baptiste Chassignet. The refrain of "He Wanted to Travel" owes a debt to that ingenious maker of metaphysical sonnets. Readers who seek out his poems "My Misspent Life" and "Consolation for my Death," in English or in French, will be richly rewarded.

CPSIA information can be obtained at www.ICGtesting.com
Printed in the USA
LVOW10s0503100815

449420LV00003B/114/P